SING

WHILE YOU'RE

Single

A self-help guide for smart women who have decided to remain single for the time being, yet still believe in the power and possibility of love.

by

L. LYNN GILLIARD

Published by: Venup Publishing/SBH Media

Table of Contents

Introduction

When I was a little girl, I would put on long, flowing dresses and dance around the house, singing and dreaming. I would dance and sing to the music of my favorite musical artists, like Whitney Houston, Janet Jackson, and Cyndi Lauper. I'd watch kids shows, like Sesame Street, The Reading Rainbow, and Mr. Roger's Neighborhood, singing along to the educational songs.

Later in life, around my teens, you'd always find me dancing around a room and humming to a tune that no one else could hear.

People would laugh at me for this behavior, but it was me. I didn't care what they thought about it.

Later on, when life started kicking me in the tail, people I thought I could count on abandoned me, things became very complicated, and I lost someone who I cared for deeply, I started to isolate myself. I stopped singing. In fact, I got very quiet.

In a blog post I defined depression as a "song unsung," and I still think that this is accurate. When you're not yourself, it's because you have a "song" inside of you that isn't being sung. It's sitting stagnant, with dust gathering. To rebound, you must find a way to start SINGING your song and face the world with renewed joy and confidence.

Even if you have to do it all by yourself.

> *"You alone are enough. You have nothing to prove to anybody."*
>
> *– Maya Angelou*

If you say this to the average person, they might roll their eyes and think, "yeah right," "oh please," "no one can really be happy as a single person," or "no one can do anything on their own."

It's a hard concept to grasp when throughout your life you've been taught to wholly depend on others for love, security, approval, and acceptance. Also, at the same time, you're constantly sent messages of low self-worth and lack of personal value. You're given almost daily messages that loudly or quietly say that you're actually *not* smart enough, pretty enough, useful enough, or strong enough on your own. You're told that you must have someone else to validate you.

Many people define their worth based on who loves or wants to be with them in a romantic relationship.

That's why so many women want so badly to be able to say that they're "taken" by someone. They want to be able to say someone else out there chose them. Someone else wanted to be with them. Someone else put a ring on their finger. Someone else validated their existence on this planet.

But what happens when they lose that someone, whether it's from a tragedy or break up or betrayal?

Then that fleeting sense of worth and value disappears, and that's what leads many women deep into bouts of depression and constant cycles of making ill-informed choices in mates. At some point, after going through these trials, a woman will be willing to take just about anything that's thrown her way, as long as she can say she has someone. *Anyone.* Some call it "low hanging fruit."

Many women don't allow themselves any time for self-reflection as a single, independent human being who is experiencing life in many different ways. They find it too scary to be alone, even for a short period. That may be a sign that you're not really comfortable in your own skin.

What This Book Is and Isn't

Nearly every book you'll read about being a single

woman will advise you on how to get a man and get married as soon as possible. Because "obviously" there must be something wrong with you if you're still single!

But this isn't that book. This is the book for women who are *decidedly* single for the time being and want to stay that way until they grow more, learn, and attract the right person into their lives. This is for women who simply don't want to settle. This is for the women who want a partner who they'll be sitting on a park bench with at 80 years old still holding hands.

The purpose of this book is not to convince you that life will be better, easier, or more fulfilling if you choose to be single indefinitely. There are definite benefits to having a companion through life.

The purpose of this book is to give you a new perspective on living as a single woman that may be contrary to what you've been taught: to settle and grab whoever you can then hold on for dear life. What I've learned over the years is that I can do many things on my own while also keeping my self-respect and sanity intact. I've learned that I don't have to spend my life seeking validation, worth, and comfort through another person to be okay.

At the same time, we do need other people to thrive. Life can feel a lot easier when you have a partner riding with you or just a really good friend to talk to now and again. It's nice to have someone who is supporting you and is there for you, especially in the hard times.

But unfortunately, a lot of women who are in relationships or "situationships" are still carrying more than their share of the emotional, physical, and mental load that comes with life. If you aren't getting any fulfillment or peace out of a relationship, what does it really mean in the grand scheme of things?

Some women choose to remain single nowadays out of dating fatigue. In my book *Let Him Chase You*, I talked about "rocks versus gems." I talked about how you must have enough sense and self-worth to pick a gem from that pile of rocks when you're dating. The problem today is that the pile of rocks has gotten so high that a lot of women are just giving up on searching—at least for the time being.

So, here's a new thought: instead of spending your time and energy sorting through a pile of rocks, why not focus more on living, learning, growing, and just allowing good things to come to you. If rocks come into your atmosphere, you just shoo them away. Ping

ping! How about moving forward, every day, trusting that the universal forces will bring someone special to you (the gem) instead of actively "looking" on dating sites and social media? And when that gem comes, you'll know it—your intuition will tell you.

Living Well

I've been contemplating the topic and content of this book for some time. I talk to and observe women who are single and not looking right now. Many are choosing to focus on living well instead. A significant number of single women are simply out of the game.

This book is aimed at those women, and those who are interested in seeing if they can successfully take a break from dating to find themselves, heal, and become more clear-minded about their goals in life.

A lot of women feel that they would have to settle for an unsatisfying, unhappy, and potentially abusive relationship just so that they don't have to be alone. And a growing portion of those women are simply not okay with that outcome for their lives.

The Guilt Trip

I watch as women fall apart because they do not have

a relationship like their friends or family members. I watch as women who are approaching their middle aged or senior years still can't get over the fact that they aren't married or attached to someone.

One of the main reasons why you may feel bad about being single is because *other people* make you feel bad about it. Then you allow that to affect and inspire your life choices. Then things start going off the rails when you make a poor choice in a companion. Then you wish you were single again.

Here's what I think we all need to understand. If you are blessed to meet a great guy and he treats you with all the respect and love your desire, that's an amazing thing. But if you don't have this experience when you think it should happen, guess what? You'll still be okay! Yes, you will!

So let's figure out how to be single and content with ourselves until the time comes that you come across your "person."

What You'll Find in This Book

Here's a thought: what's stopping you from jumping out of bed in the morning, pursuing a worthy aim that gives you a sense of purpose, and treating yourself the way you want others to treat you?

In this book, I'll tell a few anecdotal tales. These stories might help you put things into the right perspective as a woman who's single, not willing to settle, and not looking for a relationship at the moment—just learning and growing. Some of the scenarios might also make you laugh when you realize that you are not alone and that a lot of women go through these things.

One thing that I can't (and won't try to) do is take away your desire for a happy, committed relationship with a man (or woman) who will love and care for you. I don't want to take away anyone's dream—if you believe it is possible, *it is*. Period. Send it out into the Universe and wait for it to arrive. We are hardwired as women to seek a desirable mate from the time we are very young. It's also a biological inclination.

But what I can do is attempt to plant some new ideas in your head about how to best deal with life as a single woman *while you wait*. And also help you grow into a more "whole" person so that when that right guy does show up, you'll know how to maintain your power, agency, confidence, and self-respect.

The ultimate goal of this book is to give both young and older women some encouragement and tips for how we can be single and still satisfied with our lives even if a partner isn't there. I think that it's time for us to finally break free from the mentality that tells us that we are completely useless unless we are in a relationship or married by 29.

Ironically, a song gave me the idea for the title for this book, which expresses what I think a lot of women are looking to do in their own lives. To be prosperous and happy, even when they are single. Thank you to anyone who sends messages of empowerment, strength, and love to the women of the world.

I'll post that Maya Angelou quote once more to help the truth sink in a bit deeper:

"You alone are enough. You have nothing to prove to anybody."

– Maya Angelou

SING WHILE YOU'RE SINGLE

1. *You're Not Crazy*

When I was a young girl, I was taught that women are supposed to submit to men. That men are just naturally higher on the totem pole. It's in the "Good Book" after all.

My immediate reaction, as an 11-year old was, "Huh? Why?" It sounded to me like I was being taught that men were more *important* than women, and that message didn't sit right with me even at that young age. "Why can't men and women just be on equal footing?" I thought. Why am I less important than a boy my age, or a man?

I've always been somewhat rebellious and determined to walk my own path, and that definitely hasn't won me many points with the people that I know or have met over time. I'm progressive-minded and willing to challenge the norm if necessary. And when you think freely like that, people tend to call you crazy.

One way that women have been made to feel crazy is through a psychological ruse called gas lighting. If you haven't heard of this term yet, it can be defined this way: making a person seriously question their own sanity, even if they're perfectly sane, rational, and logical. The term was made popular by a film from the 1940s called *Gas Light* (an old movie that's worth the watch).

I have had countless experiences of being gas lit—made to feel like I was crazy to have an opinion that was in fact very reasonable and logical.

For example, I once dated a guy who was extremely narcissistic. He couldn't stop talking, mostly about himself. I mean, constantly talking, never allowing another person to get a word in edgewise. His opinion was the only one that mattered, and if you didn't agree with him there obviously had to be something wrong with *you.* One day I dared challenge his opinion on something very minor, and he literally looked at me like I had two heads. He immediately cut off communication with me, and even moved away shortly thereafter without telling me. He succeeded, for a time, in making me feel like I was the crazy one and that I had done something wrong. But it was exactly the opposite—he had major personal issues and couldn't handle someone who he obviously considered "inferior" disputing his opinion.

I find myself being gas lit by my relatives very often. Many times in the past I've spoken up about issues of importance, only to be told to "sit down and be quiet" in one way or another. Since I was very young, I was made to feel like my opinions were silly and worth-less, just because I was a girl. When what I said or predicted came true (which has often been the case), I was still treated like a crazy, silly girl who should re-ally just be quiet.

But I recognize gaslighting behaviors now, and I know that I'm not the crazy one—I'm a truth teller, and a lot of people just don't like to hear the truth.

Single women are gas lit all of the time. When you choose to be single for any period of time, people will question and second-guess you constantly—that includes your family members, friends, co-workers, and strangers you meet in passing. There obviously must be something wrong with you if you don't want to be paired up with someone at all moments. I mean, you must be crazy or something!

Why won't you settle for the first guy who shows you interest? I mean yeah, he has a history of frequent unemployment, constantly asks you for money, lives with his parents, cheats, and disrespects women, but at least you'll have someone.

Is it crazy to want love and respect from a relation-ship? Is it crazy to want a companion you can call all your own, rather than one who sleeps around? Is it crazy to not want to argue and fight with someone all day long like it's a sport because you're incompatible? Is it crazy to want to heal yourself and become stronger before jumping into a new relationship?

No, it's not crazy at all. And you're not crazy for simply wanting more out of life and your relationships.

* * *

For centuries, probably since the beginning of time, society has been trying to label women as unstable creatures who need to be controlled and brought to heel. Too emotional. Hysterical. Disobedient. Sinful. From the story of Adam and Eve (why did she have to eat that apple) to the Salem witch trials (if you heal people and you're a woman you must be evil) to the frequent diagnoses of "hysteria" in the late 19th century that caused women to suffer through the experiments of cruel doctors.

There's power in making someone feel like they're insane or ridiculous. They lose confidence in themselves. They start to isolate themselves. They want to be "normal" so badly that they're willing to completely succumb to another person's will, ideas, and doctrines.

Recognizing and Rejecting Gaslighting Behavior

Gaslighting is a handy trick used by manipulators to make vulnerable people feel like they are crazy or stupid. Though I'm very familiar with gaslighting, I still occasionally (albeit temporarily) fall victim to this little trick. On what planet it is unreasonable for a woman to expect good treatment? You don't have to settle for anything. Some people just don't want women empowering themselves.

Here's another gaslighting example for more clarity. Let's say you tell someone that you're single because you want a man who will treat you right. A gaslighting individual will tell you that you're asking for too much. You need to lower your standards. It's not reasonable to ask for so many things. They'll look at you with pity. They'll likely go a step further and try to scare you by saying that you're going to live with 100 cats for the rest of your life for being so demanding of *right* treatment.

But go back to the original statement for the truth. It is clearly not crazy nor out of line for *any* woman (regardless of class, lifestyle, looks, color, experience, or background) to want a man who will treat her with respect and love. Even if you'll have to wait a while for it to happen.

Gaslighting can significantly affect your self-esteem and confidence when communicating with others. It can cause you to question yourself and struggle with imposter syndrome. If you're not familiar with imposter syndrome, invest time in researching this topic. Basically, it's the feeling that you don't truly belong where you are—especially if it's in a good place or space—and that someone will "find you out."

Women experience gaslighting in so many different ways—you may have even experienced it in the workplace. Have you ever been in this situation: you raise a point that has merit and value in a meeting, but you're dismissed or ignored. Then a man says the exact same thing, maybe in a slightly different way. He's validated, encouraged, and praised.

When something like this happens, it really can make you feel like you're crazy. "Didn't I just say that exact same thing?" Yes, you did. And it was just as true when you said it. This happens a lot to women in various areas of life, and no you're not crazy. You're perfectly sane.

This is just another way that women's voices are lessened and devalued. It's a way of keeping us small and in "our places." Despite the reaction (or non-reaction) of others to your thoughts and opinions, you must learn to *trust your inner voice* and know that you are probably one of the sanest people you know. Especially if you plan to live boldly and confidently as a single woman for any period of time.

Staying Sane in This Crazy, Crazy World

Dating used to be something that was fun and exciting for women. But now it has become more like a chore. Many women are so weary of the dating process, sorting through the bad guys while trying to get to a decent one, that they resign themselves to settling for low hanging fruit.

The technology age has made dating even more complicated, as many have lost the art of conversation and don't know how to truly connect with another human being in a meaningful way. Also, since people think that they have so many "options," they are increasingly unable to be satisfied with sticking with one person.

Unfortunately, many of these societal problems are not going to be fixed overnight. It could take years or even generations to restore normal social mores and values to our culture. But in the meantime, as a single woman who has her head screwed on tightly, what are you going to do about it?

It's not easy being alone—especially when you live in a crazy world that just seems to be getting crazier by the day. You just want someone to hold you and tell you that everything will be okay.

But if you want to stay sane in a crazy world, you must learn to be okay, comfortable, and secure with yourself first.

You must also learn resilience. The ability to bounce back from disappointments time and time again, and keep moving forward—even if you have to do so on your own.

Key Thoughts from This Section

- Understand and recognize when you're being gas lit by someone who wants to make you question yourself or to make you feel crazy.

- To truly maintain your sanity, you must find balance and inspiration within yourself.

- Resilience is key.

2. Recognize and Overcome

Fear Tactics

False evidence appearing real. That's one of the most commonly known acronyms to help us understand what fear really is about. A reasonable amount of fear is healthy, because it causes you to make smart choices on a day to day basis. But in most cases, fear is an illusion that limits us from making bold strides in life.

I conquered my fear of recording my voice for my first audiobook. I boldly walked into a studio in the city one day, opened my manuscript, and just started reading *Let Him Chase You*. And it was one of the best decisions that I've ever made. From that point on, I was motivated to do everything I needed to produce and release my audiobook to the world. Then I released three more.

When you're a woman who has chosen to live single for any period of time, you can bet on hearing all sorts of scary stories from the people around you about how you'll end up. You'd better just settle down already. Your biological clock is ticking. You're going to shrivel up alone. No one will want you after you reach the age of 35.

But these are just scare tactics, meant to force you to make decisions that won't serve you well in the long run.

Take a step back and look at the people who are trying to scare you into making a rushed decision. How did their lives turn out? Do you really want to be like them?

Or do you want to relax and follow your own path?

Fear Tactics

One common fear tactic that society uses to intimidate women into settling for poor or mediocre outcomes for their lives is warning them that they will end up alone with a house full of cats.

Here's a newsflash: a majority of women (and men as well) will be living alone at some point, whether they were married or not, and probably with a cat or dog to keep them company. It's a part of life. Kids grow up and leave the nest, spouses pass on, and friends move away. And in this modern world, where people are becoming less connected due to technology, it's even more likely. It's best to get okay with the idea of living solo as early as possible so that you are prepared and still able to enjoy life's blessings (small and large) as they come.

Another fear tactic: telling women that if they put their careers first and wait to get married they are being selfish.

Is it selfish to want to create a legacy for yourself and pursue your dreams as a smart human being? Is it selfish to want to create wealth for you and future generations? Is it selfish to want to preserve your mental health and wellness by keeping your brain active and vibrant with ideas and innovations?

No, all that makes perfect sense for *any* person.

Think about the countless women who have revolutionized, innovated, and pushed the culture forward due to their contributions. Zora Neale Hurston. Marie Curie. Harriet Tubman. Sojourner Truth. Ida B. Wells. Susan B. Anthony. Virginia Wolf. Frida Kahlo. Ava DuVernay. The list is endless. Some of these women were married or paired up while some chose to remain single. Were or are they selfish or were they just inspired to live a different type of life that may have helped improve the world?

Another fear tactic used on women who choose to be single: your biological clock is ticking.

I've lost count of the times I've been asked why I don't have children. I've been asked this question by guys

I've dated, family members, people I've worked with, and the general population. I have known, since I was a very young person, that I just do not want to have children. But unfortunately, people will still make you feel like there's something wrong with you if you don't listen to that "biological clock."

As of the publishing of this book in 2020, this world is populated with nearly eight billion people, and many of them are struggling or in need. Many resources are hoarded by the ultra-rich and greedy. Climate change is a major issue that needs to be addressed. There is a lot of uncertainty in general. Having a child right now is not a requirement of your humanity or womanhood. If you decide to have a child, that's a beautiful thing and your choice. If you choose to wait to have a child, that's your choice and yours alone. If you choose to adopt in the future, that's your choice and yours alone. And if you choose to not have children for your own personal reasons, that's your choice as well.

You also do not have to explain your reasons to others—stand confidently in your choice. Design your life exactly the way you want it to be.

What are some of the fear tactics that have been used on you to make you desperate to find someone as soon as possible; even if it means you'll likely be un-happy?

Key Thoughts from This Section

- Resist fear or scare tactics meant to force you into making unsound decisions in your life.

- There's no shame in pursuing a career or aim outside of what society expects of you as a woman. In fact, you could be that person who helps change the world for the better.

- Design your life in the way you want it to be. It starts with your thoughts and proceeds with your thoughtful actions.

SING WHILE YOU'RE SINGLE

3. Shift Your Mindset

Breaking the pattern of unhealthy thinking and behaviors related to dating and relationships is an important part of living your life as a single woman who is confident, relaxed, and content. Where did you get your current mindset about relationships and what it means to be a "real" woman?

* * *

What is your mindset when it comes to men, dating, and your value as a woman? Do you believe that your life will be meaningless if you don't have a husband and kids? Do you think that it's okay if a man cheats on you or mistreats you, as long as he comes back to you every night? Do you believe that men are inherently more important than women?

If yes, where do you think those ideas came from?

What It Means to Be a Woman

Let's analyze for a brief moment what we've been taught about what it means to be a woman. Many women are taught that they are only a woman if they bear and raise children. That being a mother is the mark of womanhood, and if you choose not to do so you're selfish and rejecting your ultimate purpose. So a lot of women rush into motherhood with partners who aren't ready, willing, or able to be good fathers to meet this requirement.

And what about women who can't bear children biologically? Does that mean that they are not really women? Of course not. What about a woman who loses her child due to a tragic circumstance—she's suddenly no longer worthy of being regarded as a woman? Of course not.

Some women are taught that their main aim in life should be to get married. So they rush into marriages with partners who they barely know and who have little to offer. And many do so at very young ages, robbing themselves of important life experiences. If you talk to older women who have been married for decades, many will probably admit that they wish they had pursued their own personal goals instead of being so focused on marriage.

What have you been taught about what it means to be a woman from your elders and society? Just please remember that a woman is a woman *forever and always* regardless of what she chooses to do. Be confident that no matter what, no one can take your womanhood from you.

The Things Our Mamas Taught Us

For the most part, we learn what it means to be women from our mothers and female relatives. They are the original models for our behavior, thoughts, and actions. That's why we tend to make the same mistakes that they did in building and maintaining relationships.

I read an online thread recently that discussed how our older relatives sometimes try to get us to compromise our personal beliefs so that we can do what they did. But coincidentally, most of them are either divorced or still married and miserable. Why would they want their young daughters and nieces to do what they did when the outcome wasn't favorable for them?

The answer is complicated, and I don't think that all mothers consciously do this to hurt their daughters. I think they do it because that's all they know, and because that's what they were taught. They are afraid of what will happen to their daughters if they don't have a man to take care of them. In their generation, women weren't always able to work at stable jobs and be self-sufficient. They haven't yet adjusted to the idea that women have more opportunities now—even when they are single.

Religion adds another layer. "The bible says" is often the first thing you'll hear when talking to women who have old-school beliefs about men and marriage. Many passages also tell people that suffering is good and noble. So, it's no surprise that a lot of women choose to suffer in unhappy or abusive relationships generation after generation.

When I was young, I was taught that a woman's sole goal in life was to be married and have kids. I didn't have the insight at that time to see that this narrative was being sold to me by women who were in miserable marriages and living very unfulfilled lives. I went after this goal telling myself that I would be married by 25 and have kids by 28, blah, blah, blah. I nearly got married and did just that (twice), but I changed my mind when I started to realize it just wasn't in my best interest for a number of reasons.

From a young age, I've studied women like Susan B. Anthony who didn't want to get married like her friends, yet she lived a life that was fulfilling in terms of her career and goals. She went down in history for her unconventional choices. I think that those early influences helped me to avoid several unfavorable outcomes in the future.

Einstein said, "Never lose a holy curiosity." I think that

it's always healthy to think for yourself and question things. You have to develop your own mindset about what it means to be a woman and what you're looking for out of life. Take your time and don't let anyone, including family members, rush you into making poor choices.

Let's Talk About Music and TV

Do you know what else shapes your mindset about men, dating, and relationships? The media. That includes TV, music, movies, magazines, social media, and just about anything else that reaches a large group of people. I've written on this topic countless times in my other books, including *Let Him Chase You* (the movies that taught us to chase after relationships) and *You Matter* (the magazines and social sites that make you feel insignificant). But it's worth visiting this topic again if you're a single woman who is interested in learning more about life.

One time, while gardening, I was listening to a song by one of my favorite singers from the 90s, and I heard it with brand new ears. Here are some of the things a young girl would learn after listening to this song over and over again:

- You have to be a girl who's willing to deal with whatever her man is offering her.

- You have to be available for your man night or day and drop whatever you're doing.

- You have to be the one to make a move on the man that you want (and be willing to fight to keep other women away if necessary).

- You have to be willing to do anything a man wants sexually in order to keep him interested.

All of these messages were expressed in a catchy tune by a very young, musically talented woman. This is only one example of the many songs I loved as a teen that I've had to re-examine as an adult. It's no wonder, with messages like this in music, that a lot of young girls have questionable views about men, dating, relationships, and sex.

Television is probably the strongest form of media we're exposed to today, due to the many streaming services at our fingertips. The majority of roles played by women are "wives or girlfriends of..." This reaffirms the idea that for much of society, women only matter when they're tied to a man.

A few popular actresses have come out with insightful think-pieces about the characters that they played when they were younger. Molly Ringwald, for example, wrote an <u>article for *The New Yorker*</u> in which she discussed her role in the iconic 1980s movie *The Breakfast Club*. She admitted that some of the scenes made her cringe—especially while watching it with her young, impressionable daughter. The producer she worked with had a history of writing misogynistic stories that painted women as objects for men to use and abuse as they saw fit.

How many young women who were her age when that movie came out may have put up with poor treatment throughout their lives because of some of the negative messages they saw in movies and TV shows of that era?

On the up side, many new TV shows and premium series are starting to put women in roles that matter beyond the romantic relationships that they're in. Shows like *Scandal, Homeland, The Walking Dead, The Handmaid's Tale,* and the countless British shows that depict women in leadership roles explore the identities and life stories of women from just about every angle. They explore their private fears, strengths, skills, careers, and aspirations.

They're actual people—individual human beings who are multi-faceted. This is the content we need to consume to see ourselves and treat ourselves in a healthy way.

You know, some people look at TV and movies and say that we shouldn't take it so seriously because it's just "make believe." But when you think about it, these forms of media have shaped our culture since the first silent movie debuted in a theater. We get cues from our favorite shows and characters on how to behave in real life. Both women and men admit that the "make believe" characters they grew up with influenced how they chose to live their lives. So please don't ever underestimate the power of an image or storyline presented on television.

Don't Be Afraid to Identify as a Feminist or Womanist

Some people make light of women's movements, saying that they are pointless and have held women back.

But guess what? Women's movements have worked out for women in so many ways. From the suffragette era to the organizations inspired by Gloria Steinem in the 1970s to the womanist musings of Alice Walker to the "Me Too" movement of the early 21st century. We have learned to make logical choices to better our lives. We now have the same rights under the law and we're still making strides.

Young girls are finally seeing more positive images of women that may one day inspire them to do great things. More girls are seeking leadership positions and creating beautiful things. Women are taking leadership positions and asking for the salaries that they deserve. They are taking the reins of their lives.

And we can do the same when it comes to love and relationships. Take the reins and ask for more. Ask for what you want. Ask for what you believe you truly deserve. Let it sink in: you matter.

Change Your Mind, Change Your Life

To get to a place where you are truly okay with being a single woman for the time being, you have to do battle with everything that has taught you that a man is what makes you complete as a woman. This is not going to be an easy fight because at every stage of your life from the first time you entered elementary school to the day you started your first real job, you have been taught that to be happy, fulfilled, and complete as a woman you need to find a man.

You probably receive this message every day, whether quietly or loudly, from your parents, friends, and even colleagues at work. I'm sure you've had that one colleague who constantly talks about her "other half," then tells you with a pitying expression that you'll find your special someone one day. Reality TV shows starring women almost always show their endless pursuit of men. They would do anything to be able to say they have a boyfriend or husband to their cast-mates, including date abusive and opportunistic men. For them, being labeled single in public is worse than being used and abused behind closed doors.

What would it take for you to stop looking at these people as your influencers and simply look at them as other people who are having different experiences? Their opinions about what guarantees a happy life do not have to be the same as yours.

> *You are the only person who*
> *can make you complete.*

Recognizing a Good Guy When You See Him

As you're navigating your single life, you're still likely going to come across men who either want to date you or get to know you. This is a great time to exercise your power of discernment and start to recognize a good guy versus a guy who has major red flags.

You shouldn't give up on demanding that the partner you choose always shows you a *basic level of respect.* Here are some of the basic attributes of a good guy:

- He earns a living for himself and is self-sufficient.

- He looks at you as his one and only.

- He does not abuse you in any way, whether mentally, emotionally, or physically.

- He loves his family and treats other people with respect.

- He is mentally well. Maybe not perfect (because honestly, most people have some type of mental health issue they are dealing with), but well enough to know the difference between right and wrong.

Look over that list and take a minute to think about the women in your life. How many compromise on one or more of these things because they are terrified of being single and alone? Then ask yourself if it's really worth it to you to settle for someone who doesn't meet these very basic requirements. It's a choice that you ultimately have to make for yourself.

Also keep a balanced outlook of what a partner should be. Throughout our young lives, we have been inundated with romantic comedies, memes, and media that make us believe that a dashing knight in shining armor will show up and come to our rescue one day, fulfilling our every need.

But the truth is, *you* have to save and take care of yourself, whether you're in a relationship or not. People are flawed and get distracted or affected by life experiences. They may not be the ideal mate all of the time.

One example of this that comes to mind is Jack Pearson from one of my favorite television shows, *This Is Us*. He's truly in love with his wife and family, but still quietly struggles because of what happened to him as a child and during the war. I think that carrying the weight of the world on his shoulders all of the time ultimately led to his demise. A person just can't be all things to everyone else, no matter how hard they try. It's too much weight to carry alone—we need help from others.

Can You Make the Shift from "Boy Crazy" to "Just Crazy About Life?"

You know the feeling. You meet a new guy and every time he texts you, you smile and drop everything. It feels so nice to be getting some attention from someone new. You look forward to receiving texts from him in the morning and before bed. You spend hours browsing his social media accounts to see what he's up to, hoping he's doing the same. You've already told all of your friends about him.

But then after your second or third date, the texts slow down. Then they stop coming altogether. You text him and he doesn't respond for hours or days. It's like being high on a drug then crashing. Now you're miserable and feeling low, invisible, unwanted. Feeling bad about yourself causes you to attract another guy who's eventually going to do the same exact thing to you. It's a hurtful cycle that wears you down, and no one should have that much power over you. So how do you interrupt that cycle?

You have to get to a point where you can smile and get as giddy about something, *anything* as much as you do when you meet a new guy. Can you find a way to get high on life so that getting a text from a guy isn't the only highlight of your day?

Find an interest and pursue it consistently. Set aside a little money, like $100 (even if you have to save $20 per week), and invest in something that makes you happy. Start a small business selling handmade socks for pets at local craft fairs. If you like to cook, try a new gourmet recipe then take a high-quality, well-lit photo, and post it on Instagram. Go to your local library and sit in the sunlight for an hour reading a random book, just to do something. Go on Groupon and find a low-cost deal for a unique experience. Rent a professional camera and go make mini movies or take pictures of beautiful scenery to list for sale on a royalty-free photo site. Sit in on interesting courses at your local community college (many allow this at no cost, just ask at the front office). Go to a community service event and help out just for the heck of it. Keep yourself busy. Diversify your life. Just do something!

And don't allow a guy, or any person for that matter, to become the central theme of your entire existence for any period of time.

Need inspiration? I like to stay occupied with something just about every waking moment. I get excited about stimulating cultural conversations. I get giddy about very interesting movies and shows that explore the various facets of the human experience. I love coming home with a huge Whole Foods bag of healthy ingredients to try and a recipe to experiment with. Next to my work and writing, that's what occupies my mind the most nowadays. These are the things that I want to talk about and share with the world. If I'm talking to an interesting new person who I like, that's just icing on the cake.

SING while you're single. Find beauty in everything.

If the guy you've been chatting with turns out to be an amazing person who meets your basic respect requirements and sticks around for a while, maybe he'll get higher on your list of priorities. But your life, happiness, self-care activities, interests, and passions ought to be your top priority.

Shifting Your Energy to a Better Frequency

If you've ever watched Sci Fi movies or television shows, you may have heard the phrase "energy signature." My understanding of this phrase is that each person, place, or thing has an essence or vibration that emanates from them and can affect the things and people around them. Your goal is to be on the same energetic frequency as all things that are good and positive.

If I remember correctly, an energy signature on Star Trek was something that was specific to an individual, so that others would know who or what they are.

What is your energy signature? Is it that of a kind person? Is it that of an angry or combative person? Is it that of a deceptive person who can't really be trusted? Or is it that of a truthful and honest person who people should take seriously?

If you think your energy signature is off, the first thing you might want to work on changing is your belief that there's some kind of timeline or time limit that you must meet to find happiness or love. Other people might want you to be on their time, but you have to operate on your own time.

There's no clock ticking if you want a healthy relationship with someone. I love Tina Turner's story. When she was younger, she was rushed into marriage by an abusive man and was miserable for many years because of it. She finally escaped that hell and enjoyed her life as a single woman for many years after. She got married again at 72, and settled down in Switzerland, one of the happiest places in the world.

If you are obsessed with the idea of having children, know that you have options. Young women can freeze their eggs to be fertilized in the future. You could also adopt or foster a child in the future. Do you have nieces or nephews? Give your sister or brother a much-needed break and take them for a week. You might be very happy and eager to return them to their home after seven days! If you have a strong desire for motherhood, you will always have a way to fulfill that need.

There are a lot of kids who need some love. So just *relax*. Figure out how to get what you want without creating drama in your life.

Another way to shift your energy signature in a positive direction is to change the way you communicate and relate with other people. Here are a few points to keep in mind when you encounter others in the course of your day:

- Look people in their eyes when you're talking to them.

- Think and care about how other people are feeling in addition to your own feelings.

- When having a discussion, avoid arguing for the sake of getting your point across. Seek a resolution by seeking to understand where the other person is coming from. Sometimes you just let things go.

- Understand that some people might be going through things you don't know about, and that's why they are reacting and responding the way that they are at the moment. Have compassion.

- Be more diligent about responding to the people you care about when they reach out to you, and reach out to them more often to show genuine concern.

Communing in nature can help to shift your energy signature in a better direction as well, at least in my experience. We are natural beings after all. Go outside and take walks. Relax and sit in the sun. Talk to Mother Nature and ask for guidance.

Key Thoughts from This Section

- Take a moment to think about who taught you what it means to be a woman, and how that mindset worked out for them in the long run.

- Learn how to get high on life, so that even if you are single for an extended period of time, you're still just fine.

- Only you can complete you.

- There's no time limit on you finding love. Live to the fullest in the meanwhile.

- Consider how you relate and communicate with the people around you and make adjustments as needed.

4. Visualize Your Ideal Life

What do YOU really want out of life?

Not what others want out of your life. What is YOUR vision if you could have anything you want and need?

There's no point in asking for a better, more fulfilled life if you aren't exactly sure what that even looks like. Figure it out! You have to have a vision in mind. Clear cut details. I'll reveal a bit about my own personal vision to help you discover and clarify your own.

I've spent some time visualizing my ideal life.

I visualize my ideal place very close to a beach in a beautiful house that has beachy vibes in a good neighborhood with positive-minded neighbors. There are multiple balconies to sit on and reflect on life. There are so many lovely places to shop and just good energy in general.

I can imagine waking up every morning feeling refreshed and renewed, writing and doing what I have to do during the day to keep things in order. Hiring the people that I need to hire to help me out. Having a delicious breakfast each morning as well as a healthy lunch and dinner. having complete harmony with the people in my life who I choose to be there, getting up early in the morning or late at night and being able to walk to my local beach and just sit out and watch the sun rise or set and feel comfortably relaxed. Ensuring that my loved ones are happy and healthy and that they are doing well and are well taken care of.

I also envision having a person, once again, which is someone who I can rely upon and who I speak to just about every day whether by phone or by text or in person. Not necessarily a romantic entanglement, but consistent. And knowing that their presence at my home will always be a good thing.

You have to be as specific as possible.

A Life Imagined – Single, Content, and Satisfied with Your Choices

Close your eyes for a moment and imagine what things would look like if you were truly, completely satisfied with your life. What a happy picture. How can you frame that and put it on the mantel of your mind so that it eventually manifests into reality?

Understand that what you think about every day with consistency starts to materialize, little by little. Sometimes it comes to fruition very quickly.

You're living exactly where you want to live, whether it's a villa in Spain or an apartment in the weirdest part of Portland, Oregon.

You're healthy, fit, and feeling good physically.

You're free from the urges of desperation, so there's no pressure or urgency to find a partner.

You have one or two very good friends to share life with.

You have a team of helpers on call, to help you do the things that aren't in your capacity.

You go into your very own office, if that's best for you, decorated exactly to your liking, and do work that benefits you and the world.

You decide how your life will go and seek daily guidance from the Power of All Things That Are Good.

Have you ever seen the movie *Fried Green Tomatoes*? If not, it's a must watch. In this classic movie, we learn the true beauty of making purposeful choices for yourself as a woman instead of living according to someone else's idea of happiness. Also, we learn how making the wrong choices based on what others want for us can go wrong very quickly. It's so important that we have a vision for our own life and move toward it with tenacity and purpose.

Dare to Be Different

When I browse social media (less and less these days) or observe human behavior in action, it's clear to see that most people just "go with the flow." They jump on the bandwagon and say or do what others around them are doing. But as the saying goes, if your "friends" all wanted to jump off a bridge, do you jump with them?

Sadly, a lot of people would jump off that metaphorical bridge. But when you're visualizing a life that you want, you can't be a follower.

When I was in the fifth grade I had a wonderful teacher who spoke to us daily about the dangers of being a "lemming," and that message stuck with me. A lemming is a small animal, mostly found in the artic, and believed to be prone to going along with the pack no matter what. This led to the definition of a lemming as a person who "unthinkingly joins a movement, particularly when rushing toward destruction." In other words, they are blind followers.

The people who dare to go against the pack (future leaders) are usually ostracized and abandoned, that's why a lot of people don't want to take that risk at all.

But you may find that this is a necessary step toward getting to the life that you really want, rather than being miserable and settling in the way that others want you to exist.

A lot of women do what other women that they know do. Whether it is women in their family, friends, celebrities, or people they see on social media. Don't be a lemming—if you decide to pair up with someone make sure it's for all the right reasons.

The Truth Is Revealed with Time

When I wrote my first self-help book for women, *Let Him Chase You*, I took a different approach from the normal theme for relationship guides. Most books about dating and relationships tell women that they have to actively take pursuit if they wanted to "get their man." They blame women for having some sort of deficiency within themselves, which is why they can't find and keep a man.

Instead, in my book, I focused on providing logical information, telling women to relax and let the right man come to you. I made the motivations of both genders clear and discussed our biological inclinations (by gender and sexuality) to help women understand why we do what we do and feel the way we feel.

When it was first released, women weren't very receptive to these concepts. They resisted the idea that men should value them as prizes. Several chimed in to say that they had found their man, chased him, and reeled him in, so other women should do the same. I was a little surprised at the time to see so many women making excuses for why they should chase men to have a relationship and get married.

But a few years after it was released and beyond, women finally started to understand what I was talking about. *Let Him Chase You* is really a book about loving yourself, demanding respect, and opening yourself to attracting the right partner into your life. It's not enough to just say you have someone—you want someone who will love, cherish, value, protect, provide for, and care for you.

Being single in a world full of people who seem to be paired up can be difficult. Everywhere you look, whether it's the grocery store, social media, or at the beach, it seems like everyone else has someone. But a lot of people settle for unhappy relationships because they are insecure, dependent, and deeply afraid to be alone. If you prefer a relationship that is respectful and peaceful, you'll have to stand in your truth and be prepared to be single for a while until it manifests. In the meanwhile, sing your song and explore the other happy things around you. Every day might not be perfect with birds chirping and the sun illuminating every step you take, but appreciate the good days and keep moving forward.

Think about this: there are worse things than being alone, like being in a stressful, abusive, or oppressive relationship that you feel you can't escape. I can attest to that.

Sometimes you just have to go against the crowd and go your own way, even if it temporarily isolates you. Even if others look at you like you're crazy, stupid, or wrong. Even if you have to go through a period when you feel like no one is there for you.

Going against the crowd is not easy to do, because human beings are rigged to go along with what others do and think, even if it means they have to go against their own values and principles. Still, be strong, dare to be different, and keep all eyes on the vision that you have for your life.

Key Thoughts from This Section

- Be as specific as possible when you're defining your vision of an ideal life for yourself.

Know what you really want and ask Your Higher Power for it in clear terms.

- Sometimes you must stand on your own beliefs and standards, even when it goes against what others believe. With time, the truth will be revealed, and if you were right you can smile knowing that you said and did the right thing when it mattered.

- Follow your own path and go your own way to find happiness and peace. Just because everyone else is doing something doesn't necessarily mean it's the right thing to do.

5. You Come First

What will it take for you to realize that YOU come first in your own life?

When you say that you are putting yourself first, most people will tell you that you're just being selfish.

That might be because they have also been taught that it is somehow noble to put everyone and everything before themselves. Women are especially vulnerable to this. I guess you could call it the Superwoman Complex.

But if you look at how those people are living their lives (as well as looking at your own for the time being), how does it look? Are they always worn down, tired, and haggard? Do they always seem to be on the verge of a mental breakdown? Are they making the kind of money that they want to make to be more than comfortable? Do they even like their partners? Do they wake up excited about life? Are they living their dreams or their nightmares?

And at least Superwoman got a thank you every now and again!

Show Me the Receipts

I look at evidence rather than what people say, because to be honest what people say is usually fiction compared to the reality of things.

How many times have you heard celebrities gushing about their relationships, then you find out that they're being abused or cheated on? What about the people in your own life who are in relationships? Things are not always as they appear on the outside.

And you probably already have realized all of this by now, which is why you are reading or listening to this book. You are smart and secure in your value as a woman. If you are going to be in a long-term relationship, you want it to be full of genuine love and respect. The dating scene is difficult for women right now. But there are possibilities for the future, and in the meantime, you have to carry on with your life.

If you want to sing while you're single, you'll have to learn to ignore the people who call you selfish for wanting to put yourself first. That's the best thing that you can do for yourself and the people you love. You need to be whole before you can be a true blessing to others as well as carry on with strong, healthy relationships in the future.

What Do You Really Want from a Relationship? Give It to Yourself First

Have you ever sat back and really thought about why you have wanted to be in a romantic relationship so badly in the past? What are you looking to get out of a relationship? Here are a few possible answers:

- Love and care.

- Support in times of trouble (maybe a hug every now and again).

- A companion.

- Validation from others.

Let's take a moment to break down each of these reasons.

1. Love and care.

How can you give love and care to yourself?

I think that many people throw the word "love" around way too freely and loosely. Love is more than just a word or a declaration—it's about action. It's attention, thought, understanding, and showing up for the person you care for in meaningful ways, regularly. And you can do all of that for yourself.

Show attention and thought to yourself each day by

examining your current situation and identifying the things that you need to be okay. Be understanding of the fact that you're not perfect, no one is, and that's okay. Forgive yourself for things you've done or said in the past that you feel bad about. It's in the past— leave it there and move on! Resist feelings of guilt and shame—these are two emotions that are useless in the grand scheme of things.

Most of all, show up for yourself when it matters the most. When you need rest, get your rest. When you need to take a warm bath and relax after a long day, do it. When you need a vacation day so that you can drive to the beach and listen to the waves or walk in the park, take it. Listen to your intuition and let it guide you. Your intuition knows what you need, and soon you'll find life and love much easier to find.

This is love and self-care.

2. Support in times of trouble (give yourself a hug).

How can you give support to yourself?

When I was going through a particularly difficult time in my life and feeling alone, I nearly had a mental breakdown. I felt that I couldn't handle it anymore—I was tired, stressed, and feeling like I wanted to just give up.

Then a thought came to me. I remembered how confident, bold, and strong I was when I was a younger version of myself. I remembered how others looked at me as a leader throughout my high school and college years. I tapped into that part of myself, which is still there and will always be there. Then I closed my eyes in that moment and physically hugged myself. I imagined that more confident version of myself wrapping her arms around me and telling me that everything would be okay. And it worked.

I got a boost from that simple visualization that helped me to trudge through the hell moment that I was experiencing at the time. It was very freeing to realize that I could tap into that energy when needed to keep myself stabilized.

3. A companion.

How can you give companionship to yourself?

Is it possible that you can be your own companion? I think so. In fact, I know so. I've finally gotten to a place where I can spend time with myself and be happy. But before you can get to that place, you must first like yourself. I love me, and I think I'm pretty great. Most people can't sit in a room, at a restaurant table, or in quiet moment alone because they don't like themselves yet, and that usually comes from unfavorable experiences from childhood and past relationships.

Start spending time with yourself in safe places and listen to music, or watch a motivational video, or a beautiful vantage point with nature. And you may start to realize that other like-minded and positive people will be drawn to you. The Universe is powerful, as is the energy of Mother Nature.

4. Validation.

How can you validate yourself?

Take out a piece of paper, I don't care if it's a piece of memo paper that you tore out from an old notebook. I bought a pack of small memo pads for a couple of dollars and keep them around my house randomly. I use them often. I also have numerous pretty journals that I've purchased at crafting stores over time.

One way to validate yourself is to list everything you've accomplished, whether it's in the day, the month, or in your entire life. Then look at that list with the television off, maybe with some inspiring music playing in the background, and meditate on it.

Chances are, you have probably accomplished a whole

lot in your life, but it's so easy to forget. Know that you are an important person who matters. Always. Even if you feel that no one else sees it.

* * *

Feeling the Need to Care for Everyone Else

You must take care of yourself if you want to take care of anyone else.

We hear this all the time, but yet as women, we don't always heed the message. We're nurturers and caretakers by nature, wanting to look after everyone else. But imagine how much more effective we could be at that task if we were mentally, physically, emotionally, and financially well.

How well can you care for your ailing loved one if you're ailing yourself? How well can you raise a child (whether a daughter, son, niece, or nephew) if you haven't figured the basics of life out for yourself yet? How can you excel at work if you feel tired and drained every time you walk into the office? How well can you manage a relationship, whether it's romantic or a friendship, if you're angry and unhappy all the time because you don't practice self-care?

YOU come first in your own life!

Taking Care of YOURSELF First Is Not a Sin; It's a Necessity

I once sent a care package to someone who I knew had been going through a tough time. I went through a lot of trouble putting it together, running from store to store and arranging it just so. After sending the package priority which was not inexpensive, I texted this person at least three times to ask if they received it. Each time I was ignored. Finally, after I said I had to report the package as undelivered this person replied and said that they hadn't bothered to check their mailbox yet. After going through all of that trouble to ensure that they received the gift by a certain date, concerned about this person's well-being, they didn't even care enough to check their mailbox.

This made me think. Why am I treating another person better than I treat my own self?

In the past, I've tended to delay getting the things that I want and need. I need gifts and care packages also. So, I make it a priority to give myself little gifts whenever I get the whim. For instance, I'll put a gift card in a pretty box and put it on my desk with a message that says, "buy what you want with this" or put a bag of candy in my purse so that I'll find it later. When I see something that I really like online, I'll treat myself to it. And it's really nice to do so. Amazon allows you order things as gifts—why not treat yourself to something cute and add a gift note to *yourself*?

Taking a Good Look at Yourself

I remember looking at a photo of myself while I was on a family vacation. I was shocked at what I saw. I was 40 pounds over my normal weight, yet somehow, I didn't realize it until that very day after five or so years. I looked nothing like my normal self. I was floored.

No one I knew said anything about my drastic change in appearance, which I believe began after the tragic passing of my best friend. If I hadn't taken a good look at myself through that photo, I probably would have kept gaining weight until it was completely out of control.

After much hard work, perseverance, time, consistency, eating better foods (mostly vegetarian), exercising, and generally prioritizing my own needs, I finally returned to my normal weight.

*A side note: consistency is key. You get out there and power walk every day, eat healthy whole foods, take the meds your doctor suggests, and take approved vitamins DAILY. You'll see some results after some time.

Consistency.

In another case, I was having a heated argument with someone and happened to glance at myself in the mirror. I saw what they probably saw—someone who was very angry. I didn't like what I saw, even though I still believe my concerns at the time were valid. Yet I realized that this was not the way to resolve any matter successfully. I needed to get my anger under control and identify exactly where it was coming from.

I started going to a therapist to talk things out and doing yoga regularly. I started scheduling short trips to hotels around the area just to relax and get away for a moment. I really love that.

I started fixing up my home so that I could have a comfortable place of my own. I went to get my nails done more often, which I love to do. I started walking on trails just about every day, doing pushups and talking to Mother Nature. I did what I needed to do to feel and look better.

Sometimes you have to take a really good look at yourself, whether it's physically, mentally, or emotionally. Find out what you need and get it for yourself, whether it's a weekly therapy session, a monthly spa day, a physical therapist, or a 2-day driving vacation away from everyday nonsense. Even if you feel that something is too expensive, what I have found from experience is that when you invest in yourself and feel good, more funds tend to come to you so that you can do more of that good thing for you. The Universe will help give you what you need when you take bold steps towards giving yourself what you need.

So take a moment and think about it right now. What do you need? How can you put yourself first today?

Lock yourself in your bedroom for a few hours with the music blasting and ignore whoever is out there annoying you?

Cook a special gourmet meal, just for you?

Go to the park and sit quietly for 10 minutes while listening to the birds chirp around you? Carefree.

Take a day off from work and binge watch a good television show?

Put some time into developing a new business idea that you've been considering? Little by little the job gets done. Take your time.

It's up to you. You decide how your life is going to go, and only you. Make your own needs a top priority.

Look and Feel Good

Just because you are single doesn't mean that you should let yourself go. Your health, good looks, and happiness are for you—not just for others.

Don't ever allow a circumstance or lack of love from another person stop you from taking care of yourself. No matter how down you feel, brush your teeth. No matter how down you feel exfoliate your skin and moisturize. No matter how unhappy you feel, make sure you eat at least one good healthy meal or energy drink each day. Do a juicing cleanse. No matter how unloved you may feel, make sure your house and your surroundings stay as clean and tidy as possible.

You know why? Because a time will come when those consistent habits of taking care of yourself will generate something new and beautiful both inside and outside of you. You are constantly giving the Universe cues on how you want to be treated. You don't have to have another human recognize your efforts. Your efforts are being noticed by powers that we don't even fully understand.

It's Okay to Keep Some Secrets to Yourself

Some people think that to have a strong relationship with someone else, whether it's a friendship or romantic liaison, they must be 100 percent forthcoming. They think that they are required to tell the person everything about their lives (past, present, and future), or else it isn't "real."

I've learned, mostly the hard way, that it's not necessary or even a good idea to tell anyone *everything* about your life. It's okay to keep some personal details and secrets for yourself.

I once met and dated someone for several months who I really liked, and I could tell that the feeling was mutual. He had his own place where I would come to get away for a few days at a time. When we came together, we didn't want to part, always ate well, and had a lot of fun. His one flaw was that he had dreams of becoming some sort of rapper, despite being a highly intelligent man who could have pursued a career in computer science or medicine. I kept quiet about that and still supported him by buying all of his independently released music.

Then, one day, at his insistence, I decided to reveal to him some of my own personal dreams and accomplishments. Without much delay, he began to openly make fun of my goals—ah, the nerve! I also believe he was quietly envious that some of those goals had been achieved. This quickly caused the relationship to devolve into nothing.

In so many other cases, I've been the subject of ridicule or behind-the-back antics when I've revealed secrets or accomplishments to people who I thought I could trust. And let's not even discuss the potential energy drain of revealing your every movement, goal, or accomplishment on social media to complete strangers.

So, all in all, I've learned that everything doesn't have to be shared. It's okay to keep some things just for yourself!

Sometimes You Have to Put Others in Their "Place" When They Try to Do It to You

While writing this book, I realized something very important that I think people who want better for themselves, especially single women, really need to understand.

Sometimes, the people who are closest to you can be the biggest enemies to your progress. They expect you to stay in the same place forever, and if you dare to move forward and try to do better in your life, they'll do what they can to keep you back. That might be emotional blackmail (making you feel guilty or obligated if you don't focus solely on their needs), outright insults to make you feel insecure or insufficient, or creating drama by telling mistruths about you to others.

Just be generally aware of this, because unfortunately you can't help who you are related to and sometimes you will be forced to be around people who you don't vibe well with (like co-workers). But protect your energy and don't allow those people to rob you of your motivation, ambition, and positivity as you take steps forward in your life.

After many years of grieving and feeling down, I've finally trained myself to feel more energized and hopeful. But I find that as soon as I am exposed to certain personalities, I feel that good energy being slowly zapped from me. They call these people energy vampires. So, I make every effort to minimize the time I spend around these types of people, and very soon after I leave their presence, I'm back on track.

On another note, occasionally you'll have to set a negative person straight because they've crossed a line. I go by the mantra "choose your battles." Because if you go around checking everyone all the time, you'll also drain your energy that way.

There are some offenses that you will have to let slide.

Just laugh them off and keep living your life. Then there are other battles that will be of your choosing—especially if the offending person is a bully who constantly hurts others. When that happens, do your best to confront the person calmly and with at least a smidgen of love and understanding. That means to stay balanced, breathe, think, communicate from a place of common sense, and focus only on the facts of the matter. Don't drop to their level with insults, anger, or harsh criticism—just speak the truth and then get back to your peace.

Talking to Yourself

I find myself talking to myself often. Most people think that talking to yourself is crazy, but I think it's one of the sanest things that you can do as a human being. There are a lot of things going on in your life that other people will not want to hear about. Les Brown says that when you tell people what is going on in your life, 80% don't care and 20% are just glad that it isn't happening to them. If that isn't the truth.

So, should you keep your concerns inside, unspoken? Or should you let those concerns be known out loud so that you can feel better? Because who matters more than you?

And sometimes, even if no one cares to hear it, say it anyway. You said what needed to be said. And one day, someone might finally validate your feelings and say that you were 100% right.

I have said on several occasions that depression is a song unsung. I wrote a blog post about it, because I can relate. It is keeping things inside that you want to get out. Some things cannot be kept inside, because if you do they become like a poison. Some things can be left unsaid, but other things must be expressed.

Say what you need to say to who you need to say them to, in a respectful way of course, but LET IT OUT. Even if it is to someone you can't see. Then LET IT GO and move forward.

Who Is Listening?

While talking to myself one day, I took a step back and asked myself, "why am I doing that?"

I believe it is because I know that someone is listening, whether it's my subconscious, Mother Nature, God, the Universe, the Power of All Things Good, Jesus, or someone who cares about me who looks in on me every now and again. Or maybe I'm just talking to myself. But it feels right, and I often find solace in doing so.

Another quick thought: sometimes you have to talk yourself into things and sometimes you have to talk yourself out of things.

Key Thoughts from This Section

- Instead of relying on others to give you the care that you need, give it to yourself first.

- It's okay and necessary to put yourself first.

- Stand up for yourself and your needs. At the same time, choose your battles *wisely*. Every slight doesn't have to turn into an argument or fight.

6. Establish and Maintain Order and Balance

Don't underestimate the value of maintaining a sense of order, especially in a sometimes chaotic world.

To be content, healthy (mentally and otherwise), and motivated you must have order and balance in your life.

When you are a single woman, doing things mostly on your own, you must develop some type of order and balance in your life to stay confident and sane. Have a routine and a purpose. Take steps to ensure that your surroundings are beautiful, comfortable, and organized. This will help you feel better about your current situation.

When you are surrounded with a mess, it can negatively affect your opinion of yourself, and the results can be cumulative over time. First you begin to wallow in sadness over the way that you're living, feeling sorry for yourself and thinking that there is something inherently wrong with you. Eventually you give up on trying anything productive.

Don't allow that to happen. Put one foot in front of the other and keep moving.

Many people have chaotic lives, homes, and relationships because they have lost a sense of order. Nothing seems to be right because they can't organize their thoughts let alone their living spaces. There always seems to be something that needs to be done, whether it's a challenging assignment at work, a family matter, or a household project that you've been delaying. It doesn't help that there are so many outside forces creating negative narratives that we have to wake up and read or hear about every day.

And adding another person to the equation by rushing into a relationship doesn't help much. Now you have two sets of messy problems to manage daily.

Solutions to Get Back on Track

When the pandemic became an issue in the early part of 2020, I felt myself slowly devolving into a depressed state, again. Things were already challenging before then, and now I couldn't even leave the house to do normal things. I didn't even want to leave the bed at times.

So, I started a rule for myself to do at least one productive thing each day. It could be just getting in the shower, clipping my nails, or watering my garden for 10 minutes. At least one productive thing. And I've found that it creates a sense of order when you do that. It also often inspires you to want to do more productive things in your day. It can give you some much-needed inspiration and motivation to get other things done.

I learned that I like things to be done in a certain way. For instance, I like my clothes to be folded and clean. I like for my home to smell fresh. I like to have my hair and body products sorted into separate baskets. Sometimes even those small things can seem like a lot to accomplish when you're down and depressed.

Here's a message I received in a fortune cookie that has helped me keep things in perspective, get things done, and maintain a sense of order:

Little done often makes much.

I take it to mean that when you have a project or goal in mind that seems overwhelming, you do a little bit at a time until it's finally done. Then you can look over your accomplishments and see that it was worth every moment.

Find a sense of order in your everyday life, no matter how insignificant a task may seem. You may find that your thoughts start to become more balanced, and eventually your life starts to shift in a more positive direction.

What are some ways that you can maintain order and balance in your life as a single woman? What makes you happy? What makes you smile? What makes you feel accomplished? Here are some suggestions for getting back on track when you're feeling "out of order."

1. Set a goal to clean up just one of the rooms in your home. Dedicate yourself to this room and clean it up so well that it feels and smells like heaven. This is one of the easiest ways to get back on track when you feel like your life or day is unbalanced. Sometimes a mess around us is an indication of the mess that is going on in our minds.

2. Another idea for when you feel that things are "out of order." Step away from the situation for a while. Sometimes changing your surroundings will give you a clearer focus.

   Go somewhere, anywhere else away from the mess and just be quiet. Think about how you can get things back on track, day by day, hour by hour, or even minute by minute.

There is a story I think of from time to time when I'm facing a relatively difficult task. A physician was asked to help with a relief effort. Instead of jumping up and rushing to act, he sat at his desk and thought things through first. By the time he got up from his desk he knew exactly what his plan of action was and implemented it with precision.

Take the time to think things through before you start your new plan of action. Everything starts with a thought or an idea. *Then you do things,* such as making a phone call, or visiting someone to have a talk, or purchasing something that can help move you forward in your goal.

3. Sometimes things seem like they're falling to pieces because we don't take time out for ourselves. No matter what chaos may be happening in your day, dedicate at least one hour to something that you really love. It could be drinking a freshly made hot cup of coffee on your balcony or reading a book on a blanket set up on the grass. Maybe you have a business idea that you want to journal about. Talk to your Higher Power and ask for guidance during those times to yourself.

More Examples of Maintaining Order

If there's one thing that I have learned over time, it's that examples can help to clarify a point. Here are a few examples of what I mean when I talk about maintaining order and balance in your life.

- Ensuring that the place where you prepare your food is cleaned each day.

- Organizing your personal and business items so that you can retrieve them quickly.

- Setting alarms and schedule reminders to ensure that you keep up with your commitments.

- Bringing your vehicle in for maintenance regularly. Take good care of what takes care of you.

- Keeping a routine that ensures that you keep all of your work commitments to your clients or employer.

- Setting a diet that helps you achieve good health and sticking to it.

- Only making promises when you fully intend to keep them.

- Silencing your phone when it is disturbing your precious sleep.

- Making a commitment to accomplish at least one goal each day, even if it's just brushing and flossing your teeth.

Order and Relationships

If you want a successful relationship one day, you'll need to get things in your present life in order. It will help you be clear about what you want and what you simply will not tolerate. It will also help you to communicate with the other person more efficiently.

Note that some people will come into your life and purposely try to compromise your sense of order. They will try to implant ideas or rumors that you know deep down are not true and not right, sabotage you behind your back, and then sit back and watch you crumble—if you allow it. Be aware of these types of people, who are miserable and damaged, and keep them far away from your personal and business affairs.

You might also feel a little off balance when you hear not so great news from a person you know. You could be having the most beautiful and inspired day, then someone tells you something that you don't want to hear. Your whole mood changes. Even the way that you feel physically may change. And the next thing you know you are out of order again.

The best advice I can give you when this happens is to proceed with your day exactly as you originally imagined it. Do not allow this news to take you off course. It may be hard to get motivated again at first, but eventually you'll be able to breathe in and breathe out again and shake off the negativity.

Everything in Moderation

Have you ever heard the saying "everything in moderation?" It's possibly one of the best pieces of advice you could ever receive. It applies to just about everything in life.

Many people spiral out of control because they stop doing things in moderation. That could be eating unhealthy foods, drinking certain beverages (like wine or coffee), shopping, going to bars or clubs, having sexual relations with strangers, sleeping for days, or even exercising too much. When something becomes an obsession, it could take your life off the rails.

What does moderation mean? It means doing something in a way that doesn't disrupt your life, your routine, or the lives of the people around you. Moderation is really a key to maintaining order.

In the depths of my depression after losing a loved one (then another one a few years later), I spent an inordinate amount of time in the bed, watching television, drinking wine in a box, and sleeping intermittently. But at some point, I realized that I had to get up and do something. I started to clean up my yard first. Then I found a new part-time job nearby to distract me, even though the pay was low based on my experience. Then I started to do more things I liked to do.

I started to do things in moderation again, and it led me on the road to recovery from that depressive episode.

Limit Your Exposure to the Internet

The Internet is a wealth of information, knowledge, and inspiration. It is also a cesspool of personalities, opinions, and ideas that can throw you off balance in your quest for being comfortably and confidently single until you find someone who you truly vibe with.

I am not a super fan of anyone in particular, yet I watch and monitor stories in the media. I've seen so many pop stars, celebrities, actresses, models, media personalities, and even politicians in some cases admit their insecurities about dealing with the public, mainly due to the overreaching power of the Internet. They, the appointed "top tier" of our society, allow strangers, mostly negative trolls, to tell them who they are, what they're going to be, and how they should live their lives. Only then we have to admit that they are just people, human beings, just like us.

If someone who you look up to has that type of vulnerability, don't be surprised if you do too. It's a human trait. But we must get stronger and more resilient as technology advances and social media becomes more normalized.

*"Wake up, pick up the phone,
and read something negative."*

*Is that the best way to start
your day?*

Try not to rely too much on the Internet for your validation, attention, entertainment, education, and guidance. Take breaks from social media and pay more attention to yourself—your body, your mind, and your soul.

Instead of logging onto Twitter or Instagram, log onto *Mother Nature*. Go find a park or trail where you can walk and eventually find a place to sit down. Read a book, preferably something that energizes and inspires you. Listen to a motivational speech or audio-book. Talk to whatever Higher Power you believe in. You'll be surprised by how quickly you'll get some of your answers when you ask questions or make requests when you're surrounded by peace and quiet in nature. It doesn't matter the season, just dress appropriately, and go.

Also, be sure to get at least six to eight hours of sleep each night and appreciate your beautiful dreams.

Stand Strong in What You Believe In

As you get older, you'll learn the importance of picking a lane, a philosophy, or a credo to live by (or all three). Go with your intuition and don't let others sway you from your stance on what makes a good, happy, peaceful life.

Harriet Tubman is one of my heroines. Once attaining her freedom, she didn't have to go back to save others, but she did. 19 times in fact. Now that is bravery. She had a code and a mission, and she stuck to it. She stood strong in what she believed in, that her family and her people should be free. And guided by her strong beliefs and intuition, she succeeded.

We all need a code as well and to know what we believe in as we navigate this often-confusing world.

* * *

I think it's worth repeating what I wrote earlier about lemmings—the animals that follow each other blindly. A lot of people are lemmings, doing what others do because they don't want to ruffle feathers or be shunned from the group. They want to be liked and to mix in with everyone else.

A "lemming leader" can take you down the wrong road. You have to think for yourself and make your own decisions in life with the help of the Higher Power you believe in. And you have to believe in yourself as well.

I can't count the amount of times I've made a stance on something that most of the people I know disagreed with, or ridiculed me for, that soon turned out to be absolutely true and valid. I've doubted myself for many years, but now I stand confident and firm in my opinions and beliefs. I trust my woman's intuition; it's a gift and I treasure it.

Here's an example: I started writing this book years before its publication, but set it aside because I was concerned that women might think that it was discouraging them from seeking love and relationships. I eventually found that most of my audience were leaning in the exact direction of the purpose of this book: wanting to be single for the time being (not really looking, but still open to possibilities), purposeful, and free to live their lives on their own terms.

Another example: when I first wrote my book *Let Him Chase You*, I got a lot of resistance to the advice provided from women who insisted that it was perfectly fine to chase and pursue men. I even had a review from someone who said I just hated men, just because I wanted to empower women with common sense information. Years later, I'm getting countless messages from women of all ages who are so thankful for the knowledge and insight provided in the book.

Key Thoughts from This Section

- Maintaining order and balance in life is important for anyone, but especially when you want to sing while you're single.

- The Internet has its benefits when it comes to finding information and connecting with loved ones, but it is a breeding ground for insecurity and depression. There are millions of energies being expressed through social media, blogs, and websites that you should avoid.

- Log out of social media and into Mother Nature.

- Don't doubt yourself—do what you feel is right and stand in your beliefs.

7. Identify and Change Patterns That Don't Serve You Well

There are patterns in all of your relationships – take responsibility for them, then make changes.

The late, insightful motivational speaker Wayne Dyer told a tale about a woman who walks down a street and accidently falls into a crater. The next day, she does the exact same thing. The day after that, she walks up to the crater, sees it, and still walks into it. The next day, she sees the crater and decides to walk around it so that she doesn't get hurt again. The following day, finally she decides to walk down another street.

How many times do we have to continue potentially toxic patterns in our life before we make better decisions?

Is it a good idea to continue to find men online who are not good matches, date them for a short time, and then get hurt? Or is it better to take a break, relax, and discover ourselves so that we can be more open to finding the right people to enter our lives and eventually find the right kind of love?

* * *

I used to be so boy-crazy. As a girl, I had a crush on a different boy every year in school, and did everything in my power to get his attention. In college, I immediately started going to parties so that I could meet guys, and I met more than a few. After college, I was still boy crazy, to the point where I would even go to parties by myself just so that I could attract the attention of a new guy. Even if I was already dating someone.

Now, as I look back on all of those crushes and relationships with men, there was always a pattern. Either I chose men who didn't really want me for the right reasons, or I chose men who were very narcissistic and full of themselves. They chose me to fulfill their own needs for validation and for convenience.

I finally realized, after many different failed relationships, that I had to release that "boy crazy" energy and just relax already. How many times do you have to experience the same scenario before the light bulb of common sense turns on? Most women (including myself in my 20s), continue to jump from guy to guy, wondering why they keep having the same miserable ending.

As Albert Einstein is known for saying, "insanity is doing the same thing over and over and expecting different results."

What patterns are you repeating in your dating life? What are some of the patterns you have learned that you believe may have negatively affected the way that you're living your life today?

Generational "Curses"

We do what we do and we act the way that we act because of how we were raised, and because of the people who raised us. They learned a certain way and then they most likely taught us the same way. And if you continue this pattern, you will teach your children the same way.

This is not to say that every pattern or behavior taught to us by our parents is problematic, because some traditions that we learn are beautiful and should be carried on, like recipes, solid financial advice, being there for your loved ones when it matters, and numerous cultural wonders. But a lot of the things that we are taught by our parents are borne from fear and ignorance.

By now you have probably heard of generational curses. These are the habits, ways, and behaviors that are passed down generation after generation from parent to child then to the grandchildren and beyond. you are not obligated to continue that process. In fact, I believe that we are all obligated to break the chain and teach the children better.

One generational curse that I have seen with a lot of the women who I know is dating and marrying men who are abusive and controlling. I almost fell victim to this as well, but something within me was too strong to allow it to happen.

One purpose of Sing While You're Single is to help women avoid these types of relationships because they do not serve them or their children. Chances are, you are reading this book because you want someone who will love and cherish every essence of your being, physically, emotionally, and mentally, and be a great role model to your kids for the future. It might take some time and patience to find that person, but I believe it is possible. You have to believe it too.

Why Do I Keep Getting the Same Guys?

Many women wonder why they keep attracting the same type of guys into their lives time and time again. The answer is simpler than you think.

It's a certain energy that you're emitting. You attract

certain types of men based on how you feel about yourself, how you treat yourself, your general attitude about life, and what you think about who you are. You may also attract the same types of men based on how you present yourself to the world physically, such as dressing a certain way or wearing expensive jewelry. Sometimes you attract certain men because of the men you grew up around, especially your father.

Women are often flattered when guys boldly approach them on the street, or in public, asking for their phone numbers. But in many cases, those types of guys are "predators." They try women who they think they can take advantage of in one way or the other, whether it's for sex, money, a place to stay, or a temporary distraction. They also know that it's a numbers game—the more women they approach, the higher their chance of getting what they want.

I remember when I was around 23, I was walking down the street shopping. I was wearing designer high-heeled shoes, bag, and jeans. I had perfect French manicured nails. This guy walked right up to me, stopped me in my tracks, and boldly demanded my number. He was good-looking and back then I was attracted to bold, confident men, so I gave it to him.

He picked me up for our first date in a late model Lexus, and I was impressed.

After a year of dating and a short-term engagement (no ring) I found out that he largely depended on his mother. He was at risk of losing his car. On top of all that, he was a cokehead. After thinking over this relationship, I realized that I attracted this type of person because of how I was dressed (he thought he needed to impress me) *and* because of my own materialistic mentality at that time. I filled a need within him, and he (I thought) would fill a need I had—to be a rich guy's woman.

Women who have low self-esteem issues often attract abusive men. Women who have daddy issues often attract older men into their lives who try to control them. Women who are accustomed to being treated poorly by other people often attract cheaters and users.

How many women do you know who are in miserable relationships that they rushed into because they are insecure or tend to attract drama into their lives? This is why it is so important to stabilize yourself as a single woman before you even think about trying to be in a relationship. Work on your issues and patterns so that you can change the energy signals you're sending to the world.

And consider this. It's not only the same types of men you're attracting into your life, it might also be the same types of friends and acquaintances. After some reflection, I realized that I was attracting the exact same types of female friends to me: narcissistic, self-centered, selfish, and materialistic.

The Side Chick Lie

When there are challenges in life, we have the tendency to try to convince ourselves (and others) of things that simply aren't true to justify our actions. We sometimes make ill-informed choices seem OK to mentally manage feelings of rejection and insufficiency. I believe that is the case when women try to normalize the idea of being a "side chick." I think this is also true of women who try to normalize the idea of having a "friend with benefits."

When a man has a good woman, he has a good thing. Going to a "side chick" is like eating a microwavable mac 'n cheese cup versus having a dinner with rib eye steak, au gratin potatoes, and garlic green beans. One will fill them up for a very short time, but the other will build up his strength, vibrancy, and energy for an extended time.

The idea that there's value and purpose in being a "side chick" for any extended period of time is self-deception. And telling the world that you don't care if you're respected or have a man all to yourself is also self-deception. Everyone wants someone who's just for them, whether it's a really good friend or a romantic partner.

In today's world, some of us are so focused on reaping immediate benefits that we don't think about future consequences.

If It's Meant to Be It Will Be

Have you ever tried to force something through, get lots of resistance, and then everything regarding that situation seems to go wrong?

I'll give you an example. I called a home improvement store to have flooring installed in one of my rooms. After the measurement appointment, I didn't hear anything from them. I called several numbers trying to get information about how the project was going to proceed and find out what the quote was. They never bothered to call. When I called the store to ask for an update the lady caught an attitude with me. Finally, I realized that there was too much resistance. So, I called another home improvement store to get a quote. The quote was amazing considering the job that they would have to do, and the lady who I spoke with at the store was very helpful and took her time with me. She walked me through the store to get everything I would need. I felt relaxed in the entire process and it was done well and promptly.

If it's meant to be it will be. And it will go smoothly. You can feel when something is right or not right. It's a gut instinct that I believe we all have. Trust that because it is your intuition speaking to you.

The same is true when it comes to starting and maintaining a new relationship with someone in the future. Don't chase anyone, that has been my initial message when I started my platform.

Do not chase people, do not chase men, do not chase relationships or friendships because in a lot of cases that will likely lead you down a path where you don't really want to go. People can tell when you're desperate, and they will usually take advantage of that.

Let things happen naturally, because if you are meant to be with someone it will be easy, comfortable, and relaxed. If someone really wants to be with you, they will move mountains to make it happen.

What Else is Botherings You?

You may assume that all of your problems could be solved if only you had a man to share your life with. But if you dig deeper, what else is bothering you in your life and making you unhappy? Or *who* else? Even if you were to meet the man of your dreams, what problems would still exist in your world?

It's like they say, "wherever you go, there you are." Put it this way, "whoever you go with, there you are." If you're bitter, angry, depressed, and vengeful alone, you're going to be that way with whoever you date or marry. So instead of focusing all your attention on finding a man, isn't it better to focus on fixing those other inner problems first? There's a good chance that those other issues are holding you back from connecting with people who can help make your life more fulfilling and happy.

Maybe it's a "friend" who is draining you and making you feel insufficient or making you feel like you don't deserve good things. I have had a friend like that—in fact I had two. Both were very self-centered women who couldn't stand to see guys paying me more attention at any time.

Having someone like that in your life can do a doozy

on your self-esteem and self-confidence over time. Energy is real—being around a negative, troubled person can drain you. Get toxic people from around you.

Figure out what exactly in your life is bothering or disrupting your happiness and peace. Then get to work at eliminating the problem.

What's our goal here again? To *SING while you're single*. If you want to be happy as a single woman you're going to need to be careful about the people and things you allow to enter your life.

Will I Ever Be Good Enough?

This is a question that floats on many of our minds constantly because of our upbringing. Some of our parents make us feel insufficient from the time we are little babies. Some parents express disappointment that they had a girl instead of a boy—right in the delivery room!

You may go through school feeling insufficient because of your peers or a cruel teacher who had given up on the world. When you get into college or the corporate world, you may struggle with imposter syndrome feeling that you don't really deserve to be there. Then on top of all of that, you struggle to establish and maintain a healthy romantic relationship.

You may wonder, "when will I ever be enough?"

Even though it seems as if no one else believes it or expresses it, you ALREADY are enough and always have been. Don't wait for someone else's validation— treat yourself with the respect and love you know deep down that you deserve. Read the "You Come First" chapter of this book whenever you need to be reminded.

You Get Some of the Blame, but Certainly Not All of It

I want to end this section with a disclaimer. Many relationship experts try to convince women that they are the sole reason why they are single. But this again, is a form of gaslighting. As I mentioned earlier, obviously there are a number of flaws in their counterparts and the dating scene in general (especially online) that are causing a lot of women to opt for the single life.

You are not the only one who should take responsibility for why the dating world is so messy and confused, so be easy on yourself. You're not crazy, and you're not alone in this.

Key Thoughts from This Section

- Identify and change the patterns that may not be serving you, in your dating life and otherwise.

- Always maintain respect and love for yourself.

- In many cases we create our problems, but it's not all your fault when things don't go right.

SING WHILE YOU'RE SINGLE

8. Earn and Learn

To be a confidently single woman, you need to be earning enough money to experience life to the fullest. You must also stay committed to lifetime learning.

"Closed mouths don't get fed."

I learned this simple lesson in my 20s when I first started out writing and looking for freelance work.

Speak up and take affirmative action so that you can eventually earn the income you want. Yes, you'll likely get more than a few nos. That's normal. But you might get a couple of yes answers as well, and that's what it's all about. One yes could make all the difference.

No matter what age you are while reading this book, set a goal to earn more money from either work or residual income or investing, or doing all the above. It's also important to understand and commit to learning new things continually to keep your mind fresh and sharp. And that doesn't necessarily mean textbook knowledge—it also includes learning new life skills, like how to get along with others and how to be more effective at what you do.

Who knows what will work for you? It might be buying a cheap property, fixing it up, and renting it out. It might be writing a novel and promoting it so that it receives a continuous residual income that goes into a retirement account each month. It might be capitalizing on your best skill or talent and turning it into a profit-making venture. Consider all the ways that you can make additional income and make it work for you. You won't ever know if you don't ever try.

I'm inspired by the stories of filmmakers, writers, and professionals who didn't get their shot until they were 40 or 50 years old. It happens more often than you think. They lived a full life, went through struggles, and still had the motivation to go after their dreams. On top of that they have lived life enough to the point where they understand the world and people more, so they tend to excel in their positions.

Here's one of the best reasons for earning more income: you do not have to ask anyone for anything. You can conduct your life in the way that you see fit without anyone's input or discouragement. Of course, you want good input from good people who you trust to keep you on the straight and narrow, but there is nothing quite like having your own.

The Importance of Earning a Living as a Woman

One of my favorite motivational speakers, Les Brown, hilariously said something to this effect:

They say that money can't buy happiness. But I'd like to find out for myself!

I can remember counting change from my coin bottle at times during rough moments in the past. Being broke is certainly not something that anyone should aspire to—always have a plan for making money, saving, and being able to support yourself without depending on someone else.

Of course, money shouldn't be the only thing that matters in your life, but it sure matters a lot. Money can solve a lot of problems that hold you back and make you feel insecure or powerless. So as a woman who has chosen to stay single, for the time being, set your sights on earning an income that will ensure you can live a comfortable life.

Way back in the day, some women simply laid back on their chaise lounges, threw the back of their hands up on their foreheads and waited for a husband to come take care of them. Maybe they learned to play the piano. They weren't expected to seek education or jobs or anything productive for the future.

Many less advantaged women of the past had to get married because they were unable to make an income of their own due to antiquated societal norms and laws. They needed a husband to provide for them and their children. Imagine the stress and drama of living that life, completely powerless to make your own way.

But in present times, women have the ability to provide for themselves, and we should do so in every way possible. We have intelligence, knowledge, and things to contribute to this world. And you should be properly compensated for those things.

Seek new opportunities, teachings, and ways to make money so that you'll be successful and fulfilled in your own right. There is no guarantee that you will be catered to or cared for all your life.

I will not ever forget meeting this lovely homeless lady in New York City when I was on the way to hang out with some friends for the night. Something about her made me stop and talk to her and she told me a little bit about her story. From what I remember, she fell in with a man who she thought she could rely on and who, presumably, would take care of her. That didn't happen and she ended up having to fend for herself. She had such a gentle and calm energy despite her situation. After a long talk, I gave her a $20 bill before parting ways. I think it made her feel good to tell her story and have someone listen for a while.

You should always have a plan for how you can take care of yourself as a woman, now and in the future. It's fine to accept help when offered, but have a back-up plan.

When Opportunity Meets Preparation

When you've chosen a goal that you want to reach or a business you want to start, you need to have a passion for it and work at that goal regularly. Don't just be okay at what you do—be *amazing* at it. Be the best you can be in your field. Practice, study, and know exactly what value you have to offer the world. That way, when an opportunity presents itself, you'll truly be prepared.

There was a viral video of a woman in a subway who was approached by a game show host who wanted her to finish the words of a song. She just smiled and effortlessly sang the words, without hesitation. It was beautiful. Her hair was perfectly coifed in a flowing Farrah Fawcet style, and she was comfortably, yet stylishly dressed. It turns out she is a professional singer, and now her social following has gone up exponentially. I wouldn't be surprised to learn that she started getting plenty of offers to boost her singing career. That's a great example of opportunity meeting preparation. She was ready, and she sang her song!

There's a saying: you don't have to *get ready* if you *stay ready.*

The Importance of Getting Along with Others

I have someone who knows me in just about every establishment that I regularly visit. They look out for me and make conversation. This is because I have learned how to talk to people in a way that is fruitful instead of combative. I show genuine love and concern for them.

Some people bring their negative attitudes about other stuff that is going on in their lives to everyone around them, and it is not productive nor helpful to anyone.

Relationships are everything when it comes to being successful in your endeavors. Treat people how you want to be treated.

Find a Passion and Stick with It

When you're passionate about something that's healthy, fun, and productive, it will help you stay energized and focused on the right things.

It's a lovely and comforting thing when you find your passion. It gets you up early in the morning. It's the thing that you really enjoy doing and would probably do for free. It could be knitting, illustrating, social work, helping animals, interior design, martial arts, or cooking. It's up to you to explore these things to figure out what works for you.

When you decide to be single and not date for a while, you are going to need to find a passion for something special and interesting. When I was younger all I thought about was how I was going to find a man. That thinking held me back from a lot of opportunities to build wealth and earn a better living. I think it would have been more productive to pursue my passion as early as possible and make dating a secondary goal.

Explore!

When you see the same environment, people, and circumstances every day, it can make you think that's how it is everywhere. It's not—explore whenever you get the chance and see what the world has to offer. In the current climate, as of the publishing of this book in 2020, we're unsure of when we'll be able to freely travel internationally, but there are new places you can safely visit in your own country or state. You just have to take extra precautions.

They say that wherever you go, there you are, meaning that no matter where you decide to live or visit in the world, you'll still have your baggage with you (if you choose to carry it). And that is true. If you have an angry, bitter, unhappy mentality in one place, those emotions and feelings are still be going to be around if you relocate to another place.

But sometimes a change of scenery can be just the thing to change your perspective about a lot of things in your life. Maybe being around a different culture of people will help you relax and open up more. Maybe seeing something beautiful, like the Grand Canyon, will inspire you to pursue something beautiful.

I used to travel whenever I could in my twenties. Then for a long time I stopped traveling completely. I found myself stuck in the same place, and starting to be annoyed with everything around me.

When I finally started to explore again, I felt my world begin to open up once more. I also became more passionate about my work and increasing my income. It's good to safely visit other places and experience new things.

Reimagine Where You Are Now

I bought my first house very young with plans to get married and start a family. When that didn't go as planned, I gradually started to despise the area where I was living including the people, the scenery, and the weather.

When I started to work on myself I started to change my outlook on the area and the people around me. I started to smile more and chat people up in stores. I started to make friends with cashiers and workers at local businesses. I found a place that I thought was beautiful and started spending a lot of time there. I met new friends and started communicating and spending time with them. Soon, positive energy was being reciprocated back to me and I started to feel more like I was a part of a community. But it had to start with me.

If you're in a position where you're unhappy with the place where you're currently located and living, don't despair, or feel like nothing will ever change. Start by changing your attitude and general outlook on things. Your attitude determines how you will relate with others around you. Be kind to others and yourself.

Relax and find joy in simple, small things. Be open to new opportunities in the place where you currently live. All the while, have a vision for your future home, wherever you want that to be.

Get More Satisfaction Out of Everyday Things at Home

Have you ever woken up at 6am on a Sunday, went outside, and watched the sun rise in the distance? It's something so simple but so inspiring. I don't think we fully appreciate the wonderful things that Mother Nature provides us each day.

You don't always have to travel to faraway places to see and experience beautiful things. It's understandable that not everyone can do so due to temporary financial constraints and responsibilities. So, start looking for ways that you can get satisfaction out of things that are close to home.

For instance, there are countless websites and apps that offer low-cost hotel rates. If you need a quick change of scenery so that you can think over your life plans and goals, think about booking a decent hotel a relatively short drive or bus ride away at a cheap rate and just go there. Have a hot shower and read a book. Just enjoy being away for a while. I call them "mini vacations." It will help inspire you to take more extended trips to the places you've been wanting to visit in the future.

Rebounding

There may be times when you don't feel like doing anything productive at all. You don't want to "earn and learn"—you just want to stay in your bed, pull the covers over your head, and not do a thing. Go ahead and take those times, but use it as a time to think about what you are going to do next, because you must move forward at some point.

I spent months in the bed. It was due to grief and a feeling of abandonment. But at some point, I knew that I had to get up and I had to do something. The thing that got me back on the right track was listening to motivational books like *The Power* by Rhonda Byrne and motivational speeches by people like Napoleon Hill, Iyanla Vanzant, Stephen Covey, and Les Brown. I realized that no one was coming to save me—I had to save me.

A pity party is a party of one. If you think that feeling sorry for yourself and complaining will make someone come and help you, you are sadly mistaken. People are less willing to come to your assistance when you seem pitiful. In fact, you'll probably find that they tend to come around suddenly when you are finally doing well. A lot of people have a knack for going missing in action when you need them the most.

There's a saying that *the best revenge is massive success*. I believe Frank Sinatra said that. I may not agree with getting revenge on others, but I still understand the sentiment. It just means that you are not going to get any satisfaction by just feeling sorry for yourself and giving up. You are going to get satisfaction by taking care of yourself, picking yourself back up, and living your best life possible.

Key Thoughts from This Section

- Earning a good living and committing to lifetime learning is important if you want to live successfully as a single woman.

- Sometimes we get stuck because we feel trapped where we are living. Explore whenever possible, whether it's a plane trip away or a bus trip away.

- Keep in mind that things are different in other places. A change of scenery may change your perspective on things and help motivate you to pursue your passions.

9. Managing the Non-Single Women in Your Life

The women in your life who are in relationships, engaged, or married might try to pressure you to rush into a relationship yourself—even if it's with someone you don't feel comfortable with. How do you fend them off until you're ready to date someone who's right for you?

You'll most likely be inundated with messages that try to make you feel lacking because you are single. Those messages often pressure women to make poor choices in partners so that they won't have to be alone. They may come from television shows, commercials, social media, family members, or even just going out for a walk in the middle of the day. Everyone seems paired up, happy, and relaxed.

A lot of the pressure to find someone for yourself as soon as possible will come from your friends and acquaintances.

I once had a "friend," (I put that in quotes because in hindsight I realize that she was really just an acquaintance), who was always in a relationship with someone. She would invite me to her house to hang out with her and her fiancé. She tried to fix me up with her fiance's best friend who had strange tendencies. Of course, I resisted, and that bothered her. She wanted me to live out her idea of how I should be and who I should be with. For some reason, it irked her that I was single, and she had to "cure" it somehow, even if it meant I would pair up with a guy who was bad for me.

Eventually the relationship between us deteriorated, as you could imagine, and I had to go out on my own. I didn't have any other friends who I could hang out with at that time, so it was kind of painful to lose the one I had been spending time with for years. But now I realize that it was a blessing in disguise.

Some of the attached women in your life will cause you to make some really bad choices. You might become envious from watching them in their romantic relationships (wanting that for yourself), or relent to their efforts to fix you up with men who aren't right for you. They might simply suggest to you (openly or passively) that there is something wrong with you because you choose to be single.

One thing you will learn as you continue to travel your life journey is that things aren't always as they appear on the surface. A lot of couples are putting on a performance for the world, but the reality is much different.

Try not to envy the lives of others, because you don't really know what they are going through. It's counterproductive to compare yourself to others. Sometimes as a *singing single woman* it is best to hang out with other decidedly single women who have other ambitions. That way there is no pressure to make unwise choices.

Choose a Partner for the Right Reasons on Your Own Timeline

I have a lot of acquaintances in my life who are either married or in long-term relationships. The only thing that many of them can manage to talk about is their partners. They don't have a zest for life that reaches beyond that, which is why many become distraught when they break up or lose that partner. You should always have something else going on in your life other than just a romantic relationship.

If you get married or pair up with someone make sure that you are doing it for the right reasons. Not because you were trying to please your parents or relatives. Not because everyone around you is doing it. Not because someone is pressuring you into a serious relationship. Do it because it's the right thing for you.

Also, remember that there is no time limit on finding an ideal partner. I watched a movie about Gloria Steinem called *The Glorias,* which brought her younger and older selves together on a bus. It described her life at all those stages from a little girl to a 60-year-old woman. Every time she sat down for an interview with a man, his first question was "why don't you have a husband?" She waited until she was 60 to settle down with someone she truly loved. I also like to bring up the example of Tina Turner, who married again at age 72 after a viciously abusive marriage in her younger years. After finally divorcing her first husband, she finally had a chance to discover her true self and find happiness. Take your time, live fully, and explore.

Comparison is the thief of joy.

– Theodore Roosevelt

Almost every woman has that one friend who can't stop talking about her boyfriend or husband. Every single element of your conversation is interjected with news or information about her guy.

You could say, "can you please pass the butter." She'll say, "Oh, Richard bought me some new olive oil butter last week. He cares so much about my health."

You could say, "I got a promotion at work last week." She'll respond, "Richard's company is sending him on a business trip to Mali next month. They must really think he's a valuable asset to the firm!"

You could say, "My podiatrist got rid of that stubborn corn." She'll say, "My feet were hurting last week too. Thankfully I have my Richard. He rubbed them for me before we went to bed."

You could say, "I think I'm going to bungee off the Brooklyn Bridge tomorrow." She'll say, "no one knows Brooklyn like my hubby Richie!"

Hopefully this made you chuckle a little, because they can be some of the most irritating friends to have, as much as you may love them.

When you're in "single, not looking" mode, one of the hardest things you'll have to do is manage your relationships with women who will try to make you feel guilty, inadequate, or ashamed about not having a partner of your own. Again, remember, "comparison is the thief of joy." If you continue to expose yourself to these types of people, they're eventually going to wear you down and possibly cause you to make a poor choice.

So, How Do You Deal With that Pushy, Attached Girlfriend?

If you do have friend who is in a relationship and is pressuring you to pair up with the wrong type of guy, have a conversation with her. Just tell her straight out, "I am learning to get comfortable with being single and I just don't want to talk about that." Ask her to invite you only to affairs that are for the girls or platonic fun, not requiring a partner or pressure. When the conversation turns to "so who you are dating?" be confident and bold enough to say "no one" and then shift things in a different direction. If the women who you are with can't respect this, maybe they aren't the type of women who you should be associating with at that time.

As you go about your single life, attempting to be unbothered, you're going to find that avoiding the pressures, comments, and judgments of others may be like that famous scene from the Matrix. Constantly bending, contorting yourself, and dodging slights.

The Source of Unhappiness: Comparison

I received one of the best insights about what makes

us unhappy from a video I found online. The presenter basically said that as soon as we look at people who have what we don't have, we start to feel unhappy and unworthy. We start to wonder, "why not me? What's wrong with me?" Your self-esteem takes a hit, then you fall deeper into an unhappy place. Any feeling of lack tends to overcome feelings of gratefulness for what you already do have. It sounds irrational, but if we're honest with ourselves, we human beings can be very irrational creatures.

This is why social media can be so dangerous on a mental and emotional level—we're getting too much information about what we *don't* have.

You could be feeling on top of the world, energized, excited about life, and hopeful for the future. Then you open Instagram and there's a picture of an attractive guy and his lady, all hugged up together over a candlelight dinner. There are photos of engagement rings placed prominently. Thousands of likes and gushing comments from strangers.

The next photo is a perfectly dressed woman your age standing in front of her newly purchased mansion. Scroll some more and there's the successful 20-year old girl who somehow owns her own makeup line and claims to be a "boss." And just like that, you're unhappy, unmotivated, and you just want to climb under the covers to sleep your life away.

There are studies about this—it isn't just you who is being affected. Again:

"Comparison is the thief of joy."

Understand that as perfectly as other people try to portray their lives, the truth is usually very different. They are going through drama and stress just like you are, just in a different way. Just about anyone can get into a relationship, but after a while you might be wishing to be single and free again for peace of mind.

I've learned that many of the people who constantly, openly flaunt their happy relationships in front of single people are not as happy as they want to appear. The relationship is more of a codependent pairing. They cling to the idea of the relationship for dear life, as a source of validation.

Some women who are in relationships secretly wish they weren't. They feel trapped. If they stay they're miserable, if they leave they think they'll be miserable and alone (like you, the "sad" single girl, of course). So, they hold on to that other person they are with as a sort of insurance. In other cases, they can't get out of the relationship because of emotional blackmail or being with someone who simply doesn't want to let them go. I speak from experience here; it's a stressful thing to feel trapped in a relationship that you feel has run its course.

The Complexities of Marriage

Many married women would never admit to you that after the whole ceremony of getting engaged, showing off the ring, and finally having the big wedding party, marriage becomes extremely difficult. Many women ignore the flaws in their fiancés just to have that public experience in front of their social group and family.

But after the performance is over, real life problems begin to set in. Those flaws that were overlooked become a lot more difficult to ignore. Those dirty tighty whities on the floor don't pick themselves up, and the stains get more and more offensive by the day. The female friend he's known for over 10 years apparently isn't going anywhere. Disagreements about money start to get very real. There are many studies showing that marriage is much easier on men (See the study on this topic published at Psychology Today_entitled *Is Marriage Worth It for Women?*).

Many people settle down with the first person who presents themselves as an option. They spend years in insufferable unions, never knowing if they could have missed the opportunity to meet one of their soulmates if they'd just waited a little while longer and worked on developing themselves.

What do you want to do?

This isn't to discourage you from getting married in the future if that's what you want. Rather it's meant to encourage you to make the right choice for you *when* it's right for you. Only a commitment based on true love and mutual respect will allow a marriage to survive—it can be a very trying and complex experience. Go at your own pace.

How the Tables Turn

You may feel sad or unworthy because you're single right now and everyone around you seems to have someone. Some may make you feel hopeless by constantly bringing up the fact that you're single, labeling you a spinster or cat lady, and talking about you behind your back.

But what I've learned over the years is that tables tend to turn. The same people who may have ridiculed you could end up walking in your shoes, and you could end up with the most beautiful relationship one day. Don't ever make fun of another person's experience because no one is exempt from experiencing the same issues. Instead, support the people in your life and be there for them when they're in need.

Do an online search for "women who found love later in life." You might be surprised at the stories you read—women of all ages over 40 who took care of themselves, continued to work on their careers, stayed patient, and found long-term love when the people around them probably assumed they never would. It can happen for you too.

Maintain Your Joy

Could you get to a place where you feel content as a single woman if you actively manage to avoid people, social media experiences, and shows that make you feel insecure about it?

Could you get to a place where you can spend time around people who are in relationships and not feel envious or lacking?

Once again:

Comparison is the thief of joy.

Not allowing others to steal your joy is definitely easier said than done, but it can be done. It takes practice and time.

Key Thoughts from This Section

- Learn how to manage your girlfriends who are in relationships and set boundaries with them. Do not allow a pushy friend to force you into a dating relationship that could become problematic.

- Many of the people who you see in relationships are struggling and not as happy as you might think, usually because they rushed in.

- Tables tend to turn. You could one day become the person with the enviable love story.

- Don't let comparison with others deprive you of your joy. Everyone's life experience is different.

10. Keep Love in Your Life

No matter what your relationship status is, it's crucial that you keep love in your life in whatever way you can.

You can love in small and large ways. For example, I like to carry cat food in my trunk when I can so that I can feed strays while traveling. Sometimes I'll buy an extra health drink, water, or sweet treat for someone I see on a regular basis, like a friendly cashier. On a larger scale, I show love to certain special people I know by being there for them when they're in need, even if it inconveniences me.

I also now know the value of having at least one good, real friend in your life. It's so important to learn the difference between friends, acquaintances, and associates because it will help you to keep things in the right perspective. I've had so many women who in the past I called "friends." But in reflection and hindsight, I can only honestly label maybe one or two of the women I've known as true friends. I will expand on this more in the next section.

One way of keeping love in your life as a decidedly single woman (for the time being) is to make every effort to develop relationships with other women, whether it's for business reasons, supporting each other in your hobbies, or cultivating a genuine long-term, reciprocal friendship.

The Power of Love

When I was really low and depressed, one of the things that helped me claw my way out of the trenches was listening to Rhonda Byrne's book *The Power*. Spoiler alert, the power is love.

This book, which I listened to in audio form years ago, caused me to get up and get moving again. Eventually I began this platform, kept writing, kept promoting, and now I have a bestselling love and relationship book. I've learned that even when it seems impossible, it's possible.

Love is the key to everything. Love is the reason why we are even here. Love is the reason why you are even reading this book. We all need love in our lives in some shape or form whether it is from a family member, a friend, a pet, a random stranger who smiles at you on the street, or a hobby that turns into a passion. We need love in our lives.

So always hold on to love no matter how difficult things may seem.

Take a Closer Look at Your "Friendships"

It's important to understand the nature of your relationships, particularly the relationships that you have with other women. It's also important to understand that not everyone who you casually call your friend actually is a friend to you.

After many years of navigating dozens of relationships with other women, I've estimated that there are four main categories of people you will come in contact with:

- Associates

- Acquaintances

- Adversaries (Frenemies)

- Friends

1. Associates

These are the people who you encounter for various reasons, usually for business. It might be someone you met at a networking affair. You can only count on occasional, brief discussions related to those specific reasons, but not assistance or care for any of your personal issues. Categorize them properly and don't expect much from this type of relationship outside of business relations.

2. Acquaintances

These are the people who you may have known for a long while, but who only contact you when they need something, such as a gift for a baby or wedding shower, a supporter for a scheme they have in mind, or help when they're struggling. You cannot count on an acquaintance in a time of need.

3. Adversaries

These are acquaintances who secretly (or in some cases obviously) have some type of vendetta against you, and are determined to malign you in any way possible—usually behind your back, if they can. They will try to convince others that you're not a good person or attempt to sabotage your work. You do not want to inform adversaries of your plans. It's important that you know an adversary and keep them out of your personal or business affairs entirely.

4. Friends

These are the people who are genuinely interested in your wellbeing. They care about you, check in on you, and do what they can to help when you're in a time of need. You'll likely talk to or text your friend at least a few times a week to stay connected. These are the people who are most likely to have genuine love for you. Just as you want a friend, be a friend.

A True Friend

One thing that you are going to find as you get older is that you need at least one good solid friend who you can call on and who can call on you. With regularity.

In many cases, it can be even more difficult to find this friend than it is to find a romantic partner.

I have had countless people I've called friends throughout my life since I was in elementary school. What I've learned in hindsight is that most of them were either using me or were taking advantage of me in some way. They did not truly value the essence of me as a person, with the exception of one. That was the person I lost unfortunately.

If you find a good friend you have found a good thing. Do what is necessary to keep them around. Even if you have a falling out, take some time to think things over and when the time comes reconnect in whatever way you can. Sometimes it may be you that reaches out and sometimes it will be them that reaches out. I believe that reciprocity is the number one key in a true friendship.

Cultivate Good, Real Friendships with Other Women

When you cultivate something, it means that you take your time to prepare, tend to, and develop something so that it's ripe for growth. If you want a good, real friendship with another person you must cultivate the relationship, and it takes time.

I believe that one of the best places to meet new potential friends (remember the definition I mentioned earlier) is at your job or in your profession. The people you work with are usually like-minded and have similar goals. Best of all, you are required to see your co-workers on a regular basis so you have a chance to get to know them on a deeper level.

Now that more people are being forced to work from home due to the pandemic of 2020, developing friendships at work has become more challenging. Here are some other ideas of places where you can meet new friends and start cultivating a solid relationship with them:

- Cooperative organizations and meetups in your community that help foster connections between people.

- Volunteer initiatives (community service events).

- Group therapy with women who are struggling with the same issues you're experiencing, such as grief or anxiety.

- Classes to learn new skills, such as cooking, painting, or martial arts.

- Walking groups (women who walk trails and parks together).

You might even try to develop a friendship with someone from another country or state as a pen pal using a PO box address. At a time when everyone is pecking at an electronic device to send messages every day, it's refreshing to receive *handwritten* letters in the mail. It's something to look forward to. Just always be careful and use discretion. Again, now that in-person meetings with new people isn't advisable due to the pandemic of 2020, this might be a smarter way to connect with others in a real way. Just spray your mail with disinfectant and sit down to enjoy your letter over a cup of tea!

It could take six months, a year, or multiple years to cultivate a new friendship, but it's worth it if you believe you have a true connection with another person. Listen to your intuition to ensure you're connecting with someone who is a member of your "tribe."

And don't get offended if your new friend disappears for a little while (within reason) and doesn't text, call, or write you. Chances are, she's going through something in her own life that she's not sure how to handle at the moment. Be understanding. A lot of good people don't want to burden others with their problems, but at the same time they are going through a "dark night of the soul" alone when it would be great to have a good friend check in. Just send a message or a short, written note that says in whatever way you choose: "I care about you, and I'm here for you." It really makes a difference.

Wouldn't you want to get that from someone when you're going through something alone?

Keeping Love in Your Life

It can be difficult to rest comfortably in the idea of keeping love in your life. Especially in difficult times, or when you feel that no one is really showing love toward you.

What is love really? A lot of people say, "love you" right before they hang up the phone, or in a greeting card. But love is more than just a phrase. It's action. If someone really loves you they will be there for you when it matters the most. They act with love.

Yet even if you feel that not that many (or any) people have that type of love for you, you have to still keep love in you and around you in whatever way possible. For example, I give little gifts to strangers who I see are working hard, struggling, or putting themselves in difficult situations. I don't linger, I just tell them I appreciate them, give them a gift if I feel compelled, and go about my day. That's love.

Another way to give love is to take care of the environment. I have gotten into the habit of recycling almost everything that is recyclable. It's not convenient or always fun, but it makes me feel like I'm doing something useful. Whenever you take the time to recycle something you're showing love to the planet you live on.

One other example. If you have a family member or friend who is trying to launch a new legitimate business, the easiest thing you can do is buy something they are selling. That's showing love.

Another way to show love is to grow things. Start a small garden and tend to it. Buy a plant and take care of it. Add beauty to the place where you live. It's just a matter of planting seeds and adding water, but your effort matters a lot. You can also grow other things, like loving children, beautiful neighborhoods, and wonderful business ideas. Use your imagination.

On Faith and Hope

"Faith is taking a step even when you can't see the whole staircase." That's a sentiment expressed by Dr. Martin Luther King, Jr., one person in history who certainly walked in faith, accomplished, and will probably be remembered centuries from now for his contributions to the world. Isn't that a beautiful thing to be remembered for a good thing for so long?

I believe that we are all meant for more—a great legacy—as well. But we can't get there unless we take bold, yet measured steps. Not everyone has the courage to take a walk out on faith, which is why a small percentage of people are remembered in history.

Keeping love in your life as a single woman is a matter of faith. There are so many influences around us that tell us it's hopeless and pointless to try to love others.

But love is everything. And that doesn't necessarily mean romantic love, but love in general—for yourself, for the people you care about, for the Higher Power you believe in, for nature, and for all the lovely things around you.

After long bouts of insecurity that started when I was a little kid, I can genuinely say now that I love myself, even if no one else sees what I see. I look in the mirror and I'm genuinely pleased. That is an unconventional yet radical thing that I think everyone should try to achieve.

Years ago, I found myself in a place where I felt that I had lost all hope and was wondering what the point of life was. Thankfully, with some assistance, I was able to organize my life so that I could at least feel good about a few things.

I found a plaque that said HOPE in large letters that I hesitated to hang—I was going to toss it away. But something inspired me to hang it up. Years later, it's still hanging, and I am looking at it as I type these words. You have to hold onto some degree of hope to keep living, surviving, and thriving.

The Importance of a Purpose

A sense of purpose will also help keep you on track. A purpose is something that keeps you up at night, working late. It makes you want to keep working long past signing off time. Everyone needs a sense of purpose to keep them motivated to get up each morning and to keep working toward something.

Key Thoughts from This Section

- Love is a necessity for us, not an option. Without love, we wouldn't exist.

- Know the different types of people who are in your life: associates, acquaintances, adversaries, and real friends. Your friends are a source of love.

- Maintain some level of faith, hope, and purpose. It's what keeps us, as humans, going from day to day.

11. Remember Who You Are

Woman power is real, and it is deeply embedded in our essence as women. Don't allow anyone to rob you of that power or convince you that it doesn't exist, whether you're single or not.

What is woman power?

It's hard to describe, it just IS. It's something intangible, special, and unique. It's something that has been around since Eve, the first woman, came to be, and started bringing new life into this world.

I can't count the number of times I've had to rediscover the power that I have as a woman. Also, I've realized the power of caring about others and being decent to them—a power that a lot of women tend to possess.

68 percent of caregivers are women according to the Family Caregiver Alliance. They sacrifice their time and much of their lives to care for their loved ones.

Women have headed up protests and movements to fight injustices since the days of the suffragettes (and likely before that), sometimes being abused and losing their lives in the process.

Countless women are the lifeblood of their families, holding things together financially and emotionally, year after year. Even when it means that they don't get to take care of themselves as thoroughly as they should. Even when it means that everyone they cared for will likely leave them when they reach a certain age.

Whenever there is a problem, you can almost always find a woman behind the solution.

As much as some of these things may seem like a weakness, I believe it's ultimately a strength. Over the decades, women have made great advances in society and in their personal relationships, which I think in part is due to the resilience of women in the face of adversity and their willingness to do the right thing. I also believe that it's because of something called Karma—when you do the right thing, right things will eventually start to happen for you and the positive causes that you believe in.

Positive Vibrations

Bob Marley sang about positive vibrations. I believe that there are energetic vibrations that help make positive changes happen in our personal lives or in the world. Sometimes it takes decades, sometimes it happens in months, and sometimes it takes minutes for wonderful things to manifest. Women possess so much power to change their lives and everything around them. Use that power to sing while you're single, and to get the things you desire out of life. You can tap into that power sometimes by simply making requests and believing.

I like to walk trails and explore the outdoors. I carry a beautiful stick with me that I found years ago in the woods. I carry it partially for protection, but mostly because I really like it. One day I lost my stick and couldn't find it for days. I searched my trunk and car day after day looking for it. It was weird because I always keep it in my hand when I'm walking. Where did it go?

Finally, I just asked Mother Nature to help me find my stick. Then I did my usual exercises that day and paid homage to the beauty of nature. After a few more minutes of reflection, I put on my music and started walking back to my car. Not even five minutes later, I happened to look over at a rock along the trail and there was my stick, leaning up against it. I was elated. I still have no idea how it got there.

Sometimes you just have to ask. Remember, a closed mouth doesn't get fed. Put in a request for what you want or need, even if it seems silly, and believe that your request will be granted. In some cases, the answer may not come in the exact form you imagined, but you might receive an even better answer.

The Positive Energy that Women (Sometimes Unknowingly) Possess

Have you ever felt like people, strangers, go out of their way to be around you?

□

Even though I prefer my space, I have experienced this often. I'll find an empty spot on the beach, and suddenly someone comes right next to me to set up their spot; even when there is plenty of space. When I rode the train in New York, it seemed like everyone took seats all around me; even though the train car was almost empty.

This experience is amplified with children. Once, when I was sitting in my chair on the beach, a little boy came up to me out of nowhere and innocently asked me "are you the boss around here?" I smiled and playfully responded, "yup." In another case, a child ran into the street from his parents to try to get to me (he was okay).

All I want to do on most relaxing days is to put my music on, lay back in peace, and spend some time alone reflecting on things. But now I think I understand. They are drawn to my energy for protection and comfort. And there are a lot of women who have that same energy.

At the same time, we must learn to maintain boundaries as women, so that others don't suck the lifeforce from us. Because they most certain will if you allow it! Empaths are particularly vulnerable. Some people actively seek out people who tend to give too much of themselves so that they can fill themselves up. As someone wise said, serve from your saucer, not your cup.

As a young girl, I was timid, meek, and shy. I was also very empathetic and always trying to be there for my family members and friends. What I learned after some time is that some people simply don't and won't appreciate your empathy or compassion, and will just take advantage of those traits whenever they can.

In my books and blogs, I've written about the importance of having a strong "no." Preserve your energy and power for yourself first. Don't be afraid to say "no" with a period at the end.

"No" is self-care.

Who Are You?

You are a soul inside of a body. Your body is a physical "home" for who you really are at your core.

You are a woman who is full of potential.

You are someone who came here because you were supposed to be here for some reason.

You are strong. How else would you have beaten out so many other swimmers who were trying to make it to the egg?

Who Are You?

You are a person with thoughts, dreams, emotions, and hope.

You are a person with special talents that no one else possesses.

You are a traveler, meant to move around and experience new things.

You are a being whose voice matters.

Be faithful that no matter how hard it may seem right now, it can always get better. Approach each day with a positive mindset, even if negative things seem to swirl around you. Sing while you're single and draw good energy around you so that when the time is right, you'll meet your ideal partner and achieve your goals.

I know you might not feel like it right now, for one reason or another, but you are an amazing person. A light. A beam of love. A source of positive energy. It's just that things or people from your past or present are making you dim that light and feel like you're nothing. Yet you're everything. You're a wonderful, powerful woman.

Despite all of the things that you've been through, what you've put up with, whether it was an abusive relationship, being treated like you're lesser than, people counting you out, the loss of someone you were very close to—you're still here. And you're still doing life to the best of your ability. You're here.

And on top of that you are smart and insightful enough to still seek knowledge, information, and enlightenment. How do I know? Because you're listening to or reading this book right now. You're seeking out books and audio messages that will positively inspire you and give you a boost of energy each day.

Women are magnificent beings. We put up with so much but still manage to survive and thrive. We take care of things and people, show love even when it's not shown back, raise children (alone if necessary), and protect what or who we care about the most. We continually seek knowledge and inspiration. Despite all the pressures, requirements, and challenges that we face, we continue to grow wiser, and somehow manage to remain sane and balanced enough to push forward. Women are amazing.

Step Back and Reflect

I feel that the energy is being zapped out of a lot of women as they try and fail, time and time again, to find a great guy. Finding love is the one purpose in their lives, and when you lose a sense of purpose, you lose a passion for living. So sometimes you have to step back, take a moment to figure things out, and look for another source of purpose in the meanwhile. At the same time, you shouldn't ever give up on the power and possibility of love.

And in the face of a world where dating often has more challenges than benefits, we will adjust to that as well. I believe things will get better on all fronts, but it will take time.

Throughout history women have fought back in the face of adversity. We don't just give up and cry in a corner. It's not in our nature. We rebuild, we rebound, we adjust.

It's a Process and It Takes Time

As modern women, we've been taught for 20, 30, and 40 years or more that romantic relationships define our lives. It's going to take some time for us to shift that perception to understand that while having a good relationship with a special man (or woman) is a beautiful thing, we are the masters of our own destiny, and we define ourselves. This process doesn't happen overnight—again, it takes time.

It takes time. I've probably said that several times in this book. If you've ever taken vitamins or a remedy, you know that you're required to take it consistently for weeks or even months before it really kicks in. You can't just take a pill one day and expect instant results. You can't exercise and fast for one hour and expect to lose 10 pounds. You'll have to exercise and eat better foods regularly over a period of time before you see results. This is also the case when it comes to adjusting your beliefs about yourself and your relationships. It takes time for things to finally kick in.

In the meanwhile, remember that yes, it is possible to *sing while you're single* and to find satisfaction in your life, no matter what your relationship status is.

It's possible to overcome the challenges that you face in your life with time, patience, and understanding.

Always remember who you are: a powerful woman who is made of love. You're *everything* even when you feel like you're nothing. Explore, learn, laugh, experience, and cherish every happy moment. I love you, even if I don't know you.

Love Lynn

Key Thoughts from This Section

- Always remember who you are (a positive, high energy being full of love), no matter who may try to convince you otherwise and no matter what is going on in your life right now.

- Even when women seem to do thoughtful, caring things that make them look weak, we are still strong.

- It takes time to get comfortable with being a single woman, and to begin to enjoy it.

- We define ourselves.

- Women (you) are powerful and wonderful.

LetHimChaseYou.com

LifeLoveLynn.com

www.ingramcontent.com/pod-product-compliance
Lightning Source LLC
Chambersburg PA
CBHW060501280326
41933CB00014B/2814